heCharges against the Collector and Surveyor of the Port of Philadelphia.

REPLY OF CHARLES GIBBONS

TO THE

ARGUMENT OF DAVID PAUL BROWN, ESQ

WITH AN APPENDIX,

CONTAINING THE STATEMENT OF THE

HON. JAMES COOPER,

IN ANSWER TO THE NARRATIVE OF WM. D. LEWIS.

TO THE READER.

It became my professional duty in the month of December last, to prosecute certain charges against the Collector and Surveyor of the Port of Philadelphia, specified in the following reply to the argument of Mr. Brown, which I prepared for the consideration of the Secretary of the Treasury.

The Collector, *aided by certain individuals whose names I withhold for the present*, has since issued a libellous pamphlet, entitled, "A brief Account of the Efforts of Senator Cooper of Pennsylvania, and Charles Gibbons and their associates, to prevent the confirmation of William D. Lewis, Collector of the Customs for the District of Philadelphia, as also their attempts since his confirmation to procure his removal from office." The personal exertions of Mr. Lewis and some of his retainers, to spread his calumnies broadcast over the land, relieves me from all restraint in giving equal publicity to the evidence by which the charges against him, in my feeble judgment, are fully sustained.

There are some assertions of facts contained in the pamphlet of Mr. Lewis, which I propose to notice, briefly.

He declares that I "surreptitiously foisted into the proceedings of the commission (then closed) an argument of my own, to which Mr. Brown's was in part a reply." He also states that "it was not deemed requisite to call a single witness in his behalf." Both statements are untrue, as the following correspondence will prove.

Philadelphia, March 26, 1851.

Dear Sir:—

It has been publicly stated that, after the close of the late commission to investigate the charges which had been preferred against William D. Lewis, the Collector of this port, I surreptitiously foisted into the proceedings an argument against him. It has also been stated that Mr. Lewis did not deem it necessary to call a single witness on his behalf.

You reduced to writing, in the presence of the Commissioner, all the testimony admitted in the case, qualified the witnesses, and made up the record which the Commissioner took with him to Washington. Will you be good enough to state whether any paper or argument was foisted into the proceedings by me at any time, and also the names of the witnesses who were called by Mr. Lewis or his counsel, and examined in his presence and on his behalf?

Very respectfully,

Your obedient servant,

(Signed,) CHARLES GIBBONS.

Charles D. Freeman, Esq.,
Alderman of Walnut Ward.

Philadelphia, March 26, 1851.

Dear Sir:—

Yours of this date has been received, and in answer thereto, I would say, that I am unaware that any argument or paper was foisted by you into the Commission referred to. The only argument presented by you in writing, until the close of the Commission, (other than those bearing upon the admission of testimony or evidence,) was offered at the meeting on the day the Commissioner closed his duties in this city; to your suggestion and offer to read it, Mr. Dunlevy replied, "that he doubted the propriety of its being read, as he was merely to report the evidence, that there was not time, &c., and that he would put it in his pocket and look at it," which he did, returning it to me in the evening, to be annexed as a reply to Mr. Lewis' "Narrative."*

The names of the witnesses called and examined by David Paul Brown, Esq., the counsel of Mr. Lewis, are Geo. W. South, Chas. H. Fisler, Benjamin Robinson and Johnson Kelly. Mr. Read was examined on both sides.

Very respectfully,
Your obedient servant,
CHARLES D. FREEMAN.

Charles Gibbons, Esq,

In consequence of the absence of the Commissioner, I have not been able to communicate with him on the subject, but I have no doubt that he will confirm the statement of Mr. Freeman. The only argument which was ever "foisted" on the record at any time, was that of Mr. Lewis' counsel, which will be found in his pamphlet. They never gave me a hint of their intention to present such a paper. After it was filed in the department at Washington, the Commissioner addressed a letter to me, informing me of the fact, and requesting me to forward to the Secretary of the Treasury any reply which I might desire to make. It was a secret and defamatory attack upon my character, and was never intended for my eye, until its dishonorable purpose should be effected. I prepared my reply, and on the same day that it was presented to the Secretary of the Treasury, I furnished a copy to the counsel of Mr. Lewis, of which I hold his written acknowledgment.

The record of the investigation shows that all the witnesses named in the letter of Mr. Freeman, were examined on behalf of Mr. Lewis. During their examination, *Mr. Lewis was present, and prepared in writing with his own hand*, many of the questions which were addressed to them by his counsel. It now suits his purpose to declare that it was not "*deemed requisite to call a single witness on his behalf!*" After such deliberate untruth, it may well be doubted whether *any* statement to which he may subscribe his name, is entitled to the confidence of the reader.

He not only called witnesses in his defence, but resorted to expedients to embarrass the investigation which are utterly inconsistent with the averment of his innocence. He went so far

* This was the paper which Mr. Lewis asserts I foisted on the record.—C. G.

as to address a letter to the Secretary of the Treasury, marked "*private*," in which he assailed the character of Mr. Peleg B. Savory, the Whig State Senator, from the county of Philadelphia, applying to him the epithet of traitor, because he refused to support the native nomination of Lewis C. Levin, as a representative in Congress from the first Congressional District. Both of the Whig State Senators from the city of Philadelphia were named in the same "*private*" letter, and referred to in disparaging terms. The names of seven or eight other respectable private citizens, who had never wronged Mr. Lewis, were mentioned in like manner by him in the same letter, and the Secretary was cautioned to give no credit to their words! But he went still further. He assured the Secretary that if any other citizen of Philadelphia, should venture to make any complaint of his conduct, *he would prove to the satisfaction of the Secretary that such citizen was influenced by an improper and unworthy motive!* This *covert* attempt to prejudice the mind of a high public officer, against men whose respectability was never before questioned, was made by Mr. Lewis a few days after he had been called upon by the Secretary of the Treasury, in his letter of the 8th of November, 1850, for a refutation of the charges made in the publication of Mr. Brady, hereinafter contained! The general slander of his fellow-citizens failed in its object, *but the evidence of it remains.*

Mr. Lewis has had much to say on the subject of a certain letter written by me to the President on the 13th of Nov., 1850, in relation to some matters of general notoriety bearing upon his conduct as a public officer; and has attempted to convince the public that it was *that*, which originated the recent investigation. *He knows better! Five days before my letter was written*, he was *officially* informed that the President considered an investigation of the charges against him *to be indispensable* unless he could present a satisfactory explanation of his conduct, which he was unable to do. A reference to the letter of Mr. Corwin to Mr. Lewis, dated Nov. 8, 1850, and above referred to, will settle this point against him.

In his communication to the President, dated Feb. 22, 1851, *of which I had no knowledge until I read it in his pamphlet*, Mr. Lewis uses the following language in relation to my letter above cited.

"Having, however, thus shown the intimate connection of the letter in question with the origin of the commission that has been recently executed here, I must beg leave to quote from Mr. Gibbons' statement to the Commissioner, when called on by me to produce that letter, the following words which will be found on the records of the commission: 'Mr. Lewis may as well claim to put his hand in my pocket and search its contents, as to call upon me to produce my private correspondence which has no connection whatever with this commission.' Such a letter as that of the 13th Nov. 1850, addressed to the President of the United States, relating to a public officer, holding his commission under that President, and revocable at his will, A PRIVATE LETTER! the letter which formed the very basis of the commission, said by the writer, Mr. Gibbons, TO HAVE NO CONNECTION WITH IT! ! !"

It is not true that the statement above attributed to me was made with reference to my letter to the President. Mr. Lewis through his "amiable counsel" was modest enough to call upon me, to produce my private correspondence with Mr. Cooper, and my reply to *that call* was as above stated. But in relation to my letter to the President, I answered *in writing* (and the record will show the fact) that "it was on the files of the proper Department, and if it contained any thing pertinent to the issue, the Department could refer to it." He is a bold man who would invent and *publish* a falsehood so easily exposed!

The object of Mr. Lewis' pamphlet cannot be misunderstood. Overwhelmed with the weight of evidence against him, and unable to escape from it, he strives to divert public attention from the case, by raising new issues, bolstering himself by an array of respectable names, many of which were incautiously signed to his petitions, and by defaming the character of Senator Cooper. His attack upon that gentleman is founded on two letters written by him on the 10th of May, 1849, and addressed to Mr. Lewis, in one of which he proposed to name ten persons from different sections of the State for positions in the Custom House, and informed him that if he would consent to make the appointments, he would commence by naming George Read for the office of Weighmaster. The other letter recommends the appointment of Read. Mr. Lewis has published both of those letters, but *has suppressed* a third letter which was addressed to him by Mr. Cooper, *prior to Read's appointment*, dated the 15th of May, by which *he withdrew both of his letters of the 10th, and requested Mr. Lewis to disregard his recommendations contained in them*, including of course that of Geo. Read. At the close of the testimony *on the part of the defence*, I called upon Mr. Lewis *to produce that letter*. I now copy his reply, (made through his counsel,) from the record.

"Mr. Lewis *denies* ever having received any such letter, and he relies upon the correspondence of Mr. Cooper with Mr. Read, which has been given in evidence in refutation of any idea of any such letter having been written; and he further says that the proper preliminary to such a call would have been the proof of the existence of such a letter."

Here then, is the positive and emphatic denial of Mr. Lewis, that he ever received such a letter. By reference to the statement of Mr. Cooper, and the letters annexed thereto, marked 1, 2, 3, it will be seen that Mr. Lewis stands convicted of another deliberate untruth: the reader will there find *a copy of his own written acknowledgment of the receipt of Mr. Cooper's letter of the* 15*th, being the third letter above referred to!*

He has not only suppressed that letter and denied its existence, but he has introduced into his pamphlet what *purports* to be a copy of a letter written by Mr. Cooper to George J. Weaver, dated Pottsville, June 23d, 1849. During the investigation Mr. Lewis offered the copy in evidence. I examined it, and doubting its authenticity, *demanded the production of the original letter;* but my demand was not complied with, and Mr. Weaver *was not called by Mr. Lewis to authenticate the copy produced!* I am authorized to say, that Mr. Cooper did address *a* letter to Mr. Weaver, but he has no recollection of having written any letter which corresponds with the *copy* produced by Mr. Lewis. He believes it to be spurious: and that belief is strengthened by *the refusal of Mr. Lewis to exhibit the original*—and his disinclination and omission to present Mr. Weaver *for examination before the Commissioner, to prove that he had received such a letter.*

——"Imperfect mischief!
Thou like the adder, venomous and deaf,
Hast stung the traveller; and after, hear'st
Not his pursuing voice; e'en when thou think'st
To hide, the rustling leaves and bended grass
Confess, *and point the path which thou hast crept.*
O fate of fools! officious in contriving;
In executing, puzzled, lame and lost!"

Mr. Lewis informs the President in his letter of the 22d of February, that David Woelpper, Thomas Helm, John W. Stokes, Matthias Myers and John D. Ninesteel, "*are well enough in their sphere of life, though by no means amongst the most respectable*" citizens in the community! The Collector evidently rejects the silly notion of the poet, that "worth makes the man," and has adopted a Custom-house standard of respectability, a sort of sliding scale, of which his Weighmaster is the *maximum*, and any honest citizen the *minimum*. The gentlemen above named are engaged in mechanical pursuits:—they do not live on government pap—they can read and write—they are honest, sober, industrious, intelligent and virtuous men—and hence they fall short of the present Custom-house maximum of respectability. But there is a respectability outside of the Custom House, which the people have set up for themselves, and which every good citizen is permitted to enjoy without let or hindrance from the Collector. And these "outsiders" have great faith in the opinion expressed by a very sensible writer that, "there are two modes of establishing our reputation: to be praised by honest men and to be abused by rogues. It is best however to secure the former, because it will be invariably accompanied by the latter. His calumniation is not only the greatest benefit a rogue can confer upon us, but it is also the only service he will perform for nothing."

I have a word to say respecting the political faith of Mr. Lewis. For the first time in his life he publicly avows that he has always been a Whig, and protests that he has been a consistent Whig! He declares that he was "the Whig cashier of the Girard Bank," when the widow's mite and the orphan's inheritance were there consumed, (I pretend not to know by whom,) and that he has done all in his power "to promote the success of Whig doctrines!" When he was first dug from the ruins of that institution, it was generally conceded that he was a *Democratic* fossil. The letter which was written to General Shields in August last, by his request, and which was by him *revised, approved and mailed to the General,* and by the General received, rather sustains that opinion. A copy of that letter was produced in evidence, during the recent investigation, and it contains the following language:

"But my object in addressing you is in relation to the confirmation of our Collector, Wm. D. Lewis, Esq. I am informed that great exertions have been made to prejudice you against him, in order to defeat his confirmation, and that every species of misrepresentation is resorted to. I know no cause for this, unless it be that Mr. Lewis is not proscriptive enough to gratify all those greedy ones who seek office from him. I owe to Mr. Lewis, with several of our countrymen, a debt of gratitude for positions which we hold under him, despite the low prejudice which has endeavored to prevent him giving the smallest situation to one of us; a prejudice which is not confined to this section, but, as you will recollect, attacked even yourself. But you triumphed, and shook the bigots off, 'as a lion would the dew-drops from his mane.' And I feel sure, dear General, that you will not assist that party to triumph over Mr. Lewis, because he will not pander to their greed for place and bigotry towards our countrymen. I hope I do not too much presume on your kindness in expressing the hope that you will not be found among his enemies when his case comes before the Senate, since no good can ensue to the Democratic party by his rejection, and much injury may thereby be inflicted on the numerous Democrats he has retained in office."

But the circular which he prepared and addressed to Whig Senators, at the same time, casts some doubt upon the question. It speaks as follows:—

"SIR:—The undersigned, having learned that efforts are being made, by those who represent themselves to be members of the Whig Party, to influence the votes of Whig Senators against the confirmation of our present Collector of the Customs, for the District of Philadelphia, *William D. Lewis, Esq.*, take the liberty of addressing you on the subject, and earnestly soliciting your efforts to defeat so suicidal an attempt.

"Of the entire fidelity of Mr. Lewis to Whig doctrines, and Whig measures, as the same have been set forth and advocated by the Hon. Henry Clay, Daniel Webster and other acknowledged leaders of our Party, among whom you hold so honorable a rank, we have had many proofs, and have never heard a doubt, entertained; nor do we believe that any of those persons, who are now the loudest in denouncing him, as disloyal to the principles of our party, entertain the slightest faith in the statements which they are endeavoring to impose upon you.

"As a Whig, therefore, of the right stamp, as a zealous and able advocate of our present Whig Administration, and as an officer thoroughly competent to discharge the duties of the post, which has been most worthily bestowed on him by our illustrious fellow-citizen, now at the head of the government, we do most respectfully and most earnestly appeal to you, to vote for, and strive to promote Mr. Lewis' confirmation, and thus defeat the schemes of the disorganizers, who, to promote their own selfish purposes, or to gratify their spleen, would gladly spread disunion amongst us by his rejection."

Now here are two letters emanating from Mr. Lewis, at the same time. One, *denouncing the Whigs as Bigots*, and very strongly Democratic in its tone, and the other, very strongly Whig. I hazard no decision upon this evidence, but leave the two great political parties to determine whether either of them is honored with the confidence and allegiance of Mr. Lewis. There is one other incident in his political career which may afford them a little more light, and I will present it:—

A short time prior to the general election of 1849, and before his confirmation by the Senate, Mr. Lewis prepared an article for publication, in which he lauded *himself* for his "*great independence, impartiality, and judgment*, in the distribution of the public patronage under his control," and for "his *good sense* and *just appreciation* of the stake at issue." He concluded by reminding the Whigs that a defeat would "bind our glorious Commonwealth for seven years more to the car of *that worse than Juggernaut idol, Locofocoism!*" He placed the article in the hands of Mr. Charles Gilpin, then the Whig candidate for the mayoralty of Philadelphia, and *required* that it should be inserted *editorially* in the Daily News, as the price of his allegiance to the Whig party nominations, which were not such as *he* had earnestly endeavored to secure. A copy of the article will be found in the Appendix marked Z., with the *pithy* paragraphs italicized. Mr. Gilpin having examined it, and satisfied himself of the private and apparently selfish object of Mr. Lewis, and finding it to contain statements of a very doubtful character, which no honorable man could assert, declined lending himself to such a purpose, and did not offer the article for publication. The result was, that the acknowledged organ of Mr. Lewis in this city, edited by one of his own officers, at once opened its batteries upon Mr. Gilpin, and the Whig party, and zealously labored for the success of the "*Juggernaut idol!*" Sweet was the revenge of the consistent Whig!

I may remark in conclusion, that Mr. Lewis does not attempt *a defence of himself* in the pamphlet which he has published. He gives no explanation of the facts proved against him; he does not touch the case presented by the charges and the evidence which supports them, although he sent his heralds out in advance of his book, to proclaim that, it would be a full and triumphant vindication of himself! It is little more than a collection of calumnies and falsehoods, which can injure no man more than its *ostensible* author.

So far as it assails my character, I pass it by with contempt and scorn. Saturated with the virus of defamation, truth is so foreign to his nature, that an infinitesimal quantity of it infused into his blood would poison him. If he has wounded me in his madness, the end will probably show that, I shall be no *less* fortunate than the *man*, and he no *more* fortunate than the *dog of Islington.*

"This dog and man at first were friends;
  But when a pique began,
The dog, to gain some private ends,
  Went *mad* and bit the man.
The wound it seemed both sore and sad,
  To every Christian's eye,
And while they swore the dog was mad,
  They swore the man would die.
But soon a wonder came to light,
  That show'd the rogues they lied;
The man recovered of the bite,
  The dog it was, that died!"

Philadelphia, April, 1851. CHARLES GIBBONS.

IN THE MATTER OF THE CHARGES AGAINST THE COLLECTOR AND SURVEYOR OF THE PORT OF PHILADELPHIA.

Reply of Charles Gibbons to the Argument of David Paul Brown.

I have had the honor to receive from the Secretary of the Treasury, a copy of a document which was filed with the record of the proceedings in this case without my knowledge, entitled "Sketch of the Argument of David Paul Brown," and bearing the signature of that gentleman. I propose to reply to so much of this extraordinary paper, as relates to the subject which properly claims the attention of the Department.

Early in the month of November, 1850, the following publication was made in the Sunday Dispatch and the Daily News, two newspapers published in the City of Philadelphia ;—

A CARD.

I have been called upon by many of my friends to make known the causes which induced my recent removal from the office of Deputy Weigher in the Custom House in this city. There has been so much speculation upon the subject, and so many mysterious hints thrown out by interested parties in the case, that a proper regard for my own character leads me to accede to the wishes of my friends, and present a brief and candid statement of the facts so far as they are within my own knowledge.

When the nomination of Mr. Lewis, as Collector of the Port of Philadelphia, was before the Senate of the United States, a quantity of printed circulars, intended to be addressed to Whig Senators, were brought to the Weigher's office by Geo. Read, the Chief Weigher, to be signed and forwarded to Washington. I was directed by Mr. Geo. Read to sign as many names as I could to these circulars, and other persons in the office received similar instructions. I objected strenuously to such an act, and endeavored to convince Mr. Read that the gentlemen to whom they might be sent were too intelligent to be imposed on in such a manner, and could not fail to detect the deception if they were made. They immediately accused me of being opposed to Mr. Lewis—swore that no friend of his in this office would refuse to help him through the Senate in the way proposed, and Mr. Read handed me a City Directory, told me to take the names from that, and gave me to understand that if I refused to do it I would be removed from office. But in order to escape from the dishonorable service of signing the name of any citizen to the papers, I prepared and signed a number of *fictitious* names, but no real ones, and afterwards handed them to Mr. Geo. Read, the Weighmaster. *As he could neither read nor write,* he could not tell whether I obtained the names from the Directory or not. A large number of names were also signed by Mr. Fisler. Other persons in the office were obliged to sign large numbers of names, in order to retain their places under Mr. Lewis.

As the papers were filled up in this way, they were handed to Mr. Read, who rubbed them on the floor, or between his hands, to give them the appearance of having been handled—and delivered them to Mr. Lewis or to Mr. Norris, the Surveyor of the Port. Mr. Norris forwarded the greater part of them to Washington.

Towards the middle of October, Mr. Lewis having in the meantime been confirmed by the Senate, I heard through a personal friend of Mr. P. C. Ellmaker, the Naval Officer, that he, Ellmaker, had told him I was to be removed from office. My informant was and is a private citizen, holding no office of any kind whatever. I immediately addressed the following letter to the Collector of the Port:

PHILADELPHIA, Oct. 14, 1850.

Wm. D. Lewis, Esq., Collector of the Port of Philadelphia:

SIR—I have understood that an effort has been made by certain individuals holding office in the Custom House, to effect my removal from the office of Deputy Weigher, to which you appointed me on the 7th of June, 1849, and that they have so far succeeded, that my removal has been already agreed upon. Whether this information be true or false, I consider it just, not only to you but to myself, to state to you in this manner what has occurred to excite the enmity of those persons against me who wish to have me displaced from office.

Before you were confirmed by the Senate of the United States, I was told by Mr. Geo. Read, the Chief Weigher, and Mr. Charles H. Fisler, the Chief Clerk, that a committee was sitting in the presence of the Mayor, to take depositions in relation to a charge which had been made in the Senate, that fictitious names had been signed to petitions in the Weighmaster's Office, addressed to Senators in favor of your confirmation. They wished me to join with all the weighers and swear before the Mayor that we never saw or knew any such papers to be signed in our office. I told them I could not do so, because such an oath would be false. They insisted on my going, however, and said we must swear the matter through. I told them that no earthly power could induce me to perjure myself, but that I would leave the city and stay away till they finished the depositions, so that the other side should not prove by me that such papers had been fraudulently signed.

Charles H. Fisler afterwards offered to deposite twelve hundred dollars to my credit if I would swear as they wanted me to do. I indignantly rejected his offer, left my home, (Sept. 5,) and went to Trenton, where I remained until the depositions were finished, so that my evidence could not be taken. I refused to perjure myself, and for that reason these persons are now trying to have me displaced from office.

If there is any foundation for the statement that you contemplate my removal, I ask only for an opportunity to be heard before I am condemned. I have voted the Whig Ticket and done my duty as a Whig for twenty-one years. I challenge the most searching scrutiny of my moral character, which I believe my enemies have not assailed. On this head I refer you, with confidence, to Mr. Edward C. Dale, Mr. Francis N. Buck, the Pastor of St. Augustine's Church, of which I have been a member twenty-six years, Mr. John B. Myers, Isaac Hazlehurst, Esq., Chas. Gibbons, Esq., Mr. P. Brady, Mr. Joseph B. Myers, Mr. Robert Steen, and other gentlemen of equal respectability and character, should you require it.

On the score of my competency and fidelity as a public officer, I beg leave to refer you to Messrs. H. & A. Cope & Co., Richardson, Watson & Co., Geo. McHenry & Co., Stephen Baldwin & Co, John B. Myers & Co., S. & W. Welsh, M. B. Mahoney & Co., Earps & Randall, John Gillingham & Son, Brink & Durbin, and to our importers generally.

Confident in the hope that you will not act upon any charges that may be preferred against me, without affording me the privilege of meeting my accusers face to face,

I am, sir, with great respect,
Your obedient servant,
FRANCIS E. BRADY.

The facts stated in this letter are literally true. Mr. Fisler was the only person in the Weigher's Office, who was examined before the Mayor. I afterwards learned that *he swore the matter through.* He did not tell me where the money was to come from which he offered to deposite to my credit if I would do the same thing, and I did not inquire. Mr. Lewis took no notice of my letter, but on the 21st October, seven days after, I received the following laconic epistle from the Surveyor of the Port.

Surveyor's Office,
Philadelphia, 21st October, 1850.

Sir—I am instructed to inform you that your connection with the Custom House as Deputy Weigher, will cease from and after this day.

Respectfully, your ob't. serv't.,
WM. B. NORRIS, Surveyor.

Francis E. Brady, Esq., U. S. Deputy Weigher.

Mr. Lewis and his friends now pretend that I was turned out of office for signing the *fictitious names* to his petitions. If I had forged the names of their fellow-citizens, and covered the act with perjury, *as they desired me to do*, I have no doubt that the *virtuous* Mr. Norris would have been spared the pains of indicting his letter of dismissal, and I would now stand as high in the confidence of the Collector as George Reed, the Weighmaster, *who can neither read nor write*, or Mr. Charles H. Fisler, his Clerk.

In order to satisfy my friends that my duties, while I held office, were properly performed, I need only add the following certificate, signed by some of the most eminent merchants of Philadelphia, since my removal.

Philadelphia, Oct. 24, 1850.

The undersigned, Merchants and Importers of Philadelphia, having become acquainted with Francis E. Brady, in his official character as a Deputy Weigher of the Philadelphia Custom House, take pleasure in stating that they have always found him to be a faithful, competent and obliging officer.

H. & A. Cope & Co.
Richardson, Watson & Co.
Geo. McHenry & Co.
Robt. Taylor & Co.
Stephen Baldwin & Co.
S. & W. Welsh.
Morris, Tasker & Morris.
Nathan Trotter & Co.
M. B. Mahony & Co.
Earps & Randall.
Wm. F. Potts.
Morris & Jones & Co.

The gentlemen who have thus honored me with their approbation in my capacity as a public officer, will pardon me for introducing their names in this statement. Their testimony is too valuable to me to be withheld from the public, and I present it with a feeling of pride and satisfaction which they will excuse me for indulging.

I know that strong efforts have been made by the Collector, by Mr. Norris, Geo. Read and Charles H. Fisler, to obtain affidavits to protect themselves from public condemnation in this matter. But I believe that my own word will have as much weight in Philadelphia as theirs. If any proof is wanted of the truth of my statement, I can call persons who are now employed in the Weigher's Office, who are able to confirm it, and who dare not, as honest men, deny it.

FRANCIS E. BRADY.

The foregoing publication elicited the following letter to the Collector of the Port from the Secretary of the Treasury.

Washington City, 8th November, 1850.

Dear Sir :—

In the Daily News (a paper printed in Phila.) which was sent to me a few days since, there is a publication by Francis E. Brady, lately removed from a place in the Customs at Phila., which in my judgment deserves your immediate attention.

The facts there disclosed coming in a form so imposing and so well calculated to inspire a belief in their truth, renders it necessary for your sake as well as the character of all concerned, that a prompt and full refutation of those charges should be made public.

The disclosures of the paper to which I refer, are of a character to shock the moral sense of the public, and if the charges be true, no consideration can protect the perpetrators of such enormities from such punishment as public or social law can inflict.

I beg your immediate attention to this subject, and hope to receive as soon as your convenience will permit, a satisfactory explanation of the matter. I should add that I have submitted the matter to the President, who directs me to say that an investigation of the charges is indispensable. He, however, instructs me first to ask your explanation of the case, which, if satisfactory, may avoid the necessity of further hearing.

Truly your friend,

(signed) THOS. CORWIN.

Wm. D. Lewis, Esq., Col. Phila. Pa.

In reply to this communication, Mr. William D. Lewis addressed two letters to the Secretary of the Treasury, the first dated Nov. 11th, 1850, enclosing the affidavits of George Read, Charles H. Fisler, and John E. Murray, and the other dated on the 14th of the same month, enclosing the affidavit of Joel Zane, and other documents, to all of which I shall have occasion hereafter to refer.

The explanation of Mr. Lewis not being satisfactory to the President or the Department, Mr. A. H. Dunlevy, of Ohio, was commissioned to proceed to Philadelphia, and examine witnesses in the case. He was instructed to confine the testimony to two specifications, as follows, to wit:

1. The Collector of the Port of Philadelphia is guilty of a want of fidelity to the Government, and to the character of the present National Administration, by retaining in the office of Weigh-master a person whom he has always known to be incompetent for the proper performance of the duties of the said office, and who stands charged with perjury on the Legislative records of Pennsylvania, a fact well known to the Collector at the time that he appointed him to the said office.

2. The Collector and Surveyor of the Port of Philadelphia were instrumental in procuring fictitious signatures to certain printed letters addressed to members of the Senate of the United States, urging the confirmation of the said Collector whose name was then before the Senate, and that said signatures were obtained through the Weigh-master, acting in the matter with their knowledge and consent, and that said letters were forwarded as genuine letters to certain Senators by the said Collector and Surveyor of the Port of Philadelphia.

All the testimony which was taken in the case, has been duly returned to the Department by the Commissioner, and the question remains to be decided, how far does it sustain the charges against the officers named.

The first part of the first specification, relates to the competency of the Weigh-master, George Read, and upon this point Mr. Brown, in his argument, declares as follows, to wit: "As to Mr. Read's incompetency to fulfil the duties of his office, *he has given abundant proofs to the contrary*, since he has held the office; and upon the evidence, has suffered nothing in comparison with any of his predecessors; and he has exhibited testimonials of his entire competency and ability, from sources the most satisfactory and responsible. Merchants, whose dealings led them into perfect familiarity with the office of Weigher, and who, therefore, were competent to decide upon the fidelity and efficiency of the incumbent." I answer this, by presenting some of Mr. Brown's "abundant proofs" on this point. And first, I will permit Mr. Read, the Weigh-master, to speak for himself. In his examination will be found the following questions, objections and answers:

Q. About what are the annual expenses of your office?

A. I can't tell. *I can tell the monthly expenses, I can tell what I paid to-day,* they are sometimes more and sometimes less.

Q. Well, what did you pay to-day?

A. I paid eight hundred and fifty dollars, sir, to-day, and on Saturday, I shall have to pay some more for transient laborers.

Q. What would the annual expenses amount to at the rate of eight hundred and fifty dollars a month?

A. I suppose you don't exactly want me to calculate it, you are a better hand at doing that yourself than I am. *I can't exactly tell.*

Q. Try and tell me what they would amount to at the rate mentioned?

A. I decline answering it, sir.

Q. Are you able to answer it?

(*Mr. Brown objects to the question, and the question is overruled, because the witness has already answered as far as he can the expenditures of the department;* and if intended to discredit the witness it is incompetent, as he is their own witness.)

Q. What were the expenses of your department during the last year?

(*Objected to by Mr. Brown, and question overruled.*)

* * * * * * *

Q. What amount is paid monthly, on an average, to the laborers, *from whom you take no receipts?*

(*Objected to by Mr. Brown, and question overruled.*)

Q. What amount of money do you disburse monthly for which you take no vouchers?

(*Objected to by Mr. Brown, and question overruled.*)

* * * * * * *

Q. How do you know that Exhibit No. 2, is not one of the letters which you sent to Mr. Lewis?

A. By the language, sir, what contains in the letter.

Q. Can you *read* that letter, sir?

(*Objected to by Mr. Brown.* Objection overruled by the Commissioner.)

A. If I had time, very like I could read it.

Will you be good enough to read it to the Commissioner?

(Question overruled by the Commissioner, as leading to an examination we have no right to make, and no mode of testing.)

Q. Can you now state what is contained in that letter by which you identify it? (Letter placed in the hands of the witness.)

A. I decline answering that question.

Question repeated.

A. I know that it is the letter *by Mr. Brown reading it there this moment.*

Q. I suppose you know it in no other way?

A. Oh yes, sir, I know it by the language—*hearing it read so often.*

John E. Murray is a deputy weigher in the Customs, and holds his office at the will of Mr. Lewis. It will be observed, that he testified with great reluctance, and with a strong mental bias in favor of his employer. On the question of the competency of Geo. Read, he answered as follows:

Q. State, according to the best of your knowledge, whether George Read is able to read or write more than his own name.

(*Question objected to by Mr. Brown,* and objection overruled by the Commissioner.)

A. If I make my answer from that of knowledge derived from circumstances, I should say he could not, and the circumstances are, the fact of his asking others to read and to write for him. * *

Being cross-examined by Mr. Brown on this point, the witness was asked,

Q. Was not Mr. Read defective in his sight, did he not wear spectacles?

A. I think he was; he wears specs. sometimes.

Joel Zane, also a deputy weigher, testifies as follows:

Q. Is he (Geo. Read) able to write any name but his own?

A. I cannot say, but I have never seen him write any thing but his own name.

Q. Do you know whether he is capable of keeping an account?

A. I do not.

Q. Is it not quite notorious that he can neither read nor write more than his own name?

(*Question objected to by Mr. Brown, and overruled by the Commissioner.*)

Q. To the best of your knowledge and belief, is George Read able to read or write more than his own name?

Objected to by Mr. Brown. Question overruled by the Commissioner, and witness directed to state any facts from which he forms his own opinion that Mr. Read is unable to read or write, or otherwise. Witness answers, "From the circumstance of never seeing him read a note brought into the office for him but hand it to some person in the office to read. I never saw him read a note, bill or any thing of the kind: he always called upon Mr. Fisler or myself or some person in the office to read to him—*to tell him what the contents were.* I mean to convey by my answer, that they should tell him what the contents were. Those are the grounds on which I believe that he cannot read. The grounds on which I believe that he cannot write are, that I have never seen him write anything but his own name, but always employed some person in the office to write notes, and answer notes and letters for him. This I have seen repeatedly done by Mr. Fisler."

Q. Did you ever know George Read to keep an account of the cargo of any vessel which has ever entered this port since his appointment?

A. I never have.

Mr. Zane was not cross-examined on this point.

FRANCIS E. BRADY says in his testimony, "he, (George Read,) can *neither read nor write, nor spell the name of any vessel in the Port of Philadelphia.*

MR. GEORGE W. SOUTH, the first witness called for the defendant, is the confidential friend of George Read. The nature and extent of the extraordinary intimacy which has existed between these two individuals, for some twelve years, may be inferred from the report of the Committee of the Pennsylvania Legislature, appointed to inquire into charges of bribery and corruption against certain banks. The report was made in 1842, and the letters which Read caused to be written for himself, and addressed to Mr. South, for the purpose, as he admits, of extorting money from the Bank of the United States, and the use which Mr. South made of those letters, fully appear in the Journal of the House of Representatives of Pennsylvania, which accompanies the evidence.

Although Mr. South, in his examination-in-chief, was permitted to prove that Read had been elected County Treasurer in 1840, by the County Board, yet on his cross-examination, when he was asked as to the extent of his own participation in that proceeding, objections were raised by the counsel of Mr. Lewis, and the offer was overruled. It is shown, however, that after Read's election to that office, he appointed South his deputy, by whom the duties of the office were performed. The disposition of South to equivocate during his cross-examination, his reluctance in giving adverse evidence, and his evasive replies, are worthy of observation.

He was asked,

Who performed the duties of County Treasurer during the term for which George Read was elected?

Question objected to by Mr. Brown.

Objection overruled.

A. After his election, sir, he appointed me his deputy.

Q. Did you discharge all the duties of the office?

A. He appointed me to have a supervision of the office and to perform such duties as *I thought proper to perform.* Mr. Read was constantly there himself.

Q. Did you not perfom all the duties of the office?

A. I did not keep the books, nor anything of that kind.

Q. Mr. South, you know perfectly well what is meant, and you will please to answer the question.

A. I performed all the duties of the Cashier of the office.

Q. What part of the dutics did Read perform ?

A. He used to pay out moneys on orders from the County Commissioners.

Q. Who read those orders to him ?

A. I don't know, sir—He could understand the *figures* on those orders as well as I could.

Q. Was he able to read the orders ?

A. He was not able to read the orders *without considerable viewing of it, and then he could make it out; it must have been written very plainly, too, to enable him to do it.*

Q. Are you willing to say, sir, upon the oath which you have taken, that George Read was at that time acquainted with the lettters of the alphabet ?

A. I *think* he was—with the *letters* of the alphabet.

This course of cross-examination was here objected to by the Counsel of Mr. Lewis, and overruled by the Commissioner.

JOHNSTON KELLY, *a laborer* connected with the Weigher's department was next called by the counsel of Mr. Lewis, and examined in chief on the question of Read's competency.—He testified that he had been attached to the office while Mr. Grund was Weigh-master.

Q. Having had a knowledge of the office as held by different incumbents, will you state what were the attentions and promptitude and conduct in that office by Mr. Read.

A. Well—I seen Mr. Read there daily.

Q. Prompt and punctual in his payments ?

A. Yes, sir.

Q. Well, how did he compare with the other officers, Weighmasters that you have known there; was he equal to them or otherwise in his attentions to his duties ?

A. He attended more to his duties than any of the other two Weighmasters who was there during my time.—I never heard any complaint against him.

On his cross-examination this witness stated in reply to the question, "You are a better scholar than Read, are you not ?"

A. Well, I don't know. I can write and read a little.

Q. Can George Read do that ?

A. *Yes, sir, I have seen him writing.*

Q. Did you ever see him write more than his own name ?

A. *No, sir;* except putting down with a pencil the weights once. He wrote his name to a check *most splendid,* and I went to the Bank with it. I saw him once put down "85" or "80," I am not sure which, with a pencil. I don't know whether he can read or not.

(It has been proved by other witnesses that Read always had his checks filled up for him by other persons.)

Charles H. Fisler was the next witness examined on this point on the part of the defence. He testified that he had been employed in the Weigher's office since **1836**, with the exception of a year and a half, and that he is entirely familiar with the machinery and duties of the office. The following questions were then addressed to him by the counsel of Mr. Lewis.

Q. Now, sir, with that knowledge, will you say whether George Read since he has been the incumbent has or has not been a *competent and efficient officer?*

A. *He has, sir.*

Q. Is he regular in his attendance?

A. Yes, sir.

Q. Careful in his settlements?

A. Yes, sir.

Q. What are the duties, sir, appropriate to the Weigher?

A. *His duty is to oversee the whole department and see that every thing goes on right.*

Q. To the best of your observation and knowledge, how does Mr. Read compare in that respect with any of his predecessors?

A. I think he is more attentive than any Weigher we have ever had since George Guier's administration?

On his cross-examination this witness testified as follows:

Q. Can George Read read or write more than his own name?

A. *I think he can, sir.*

Q. Did you ever see him write more than his own name?

A. *I did, sir.*

Q. What, and when, and where?

A. I have seen him pick up a pen at my desk and write a *syllable, or something or other, bnt I don't know what it was, whether the word Philadelphia or not; I never saw him write a letter.*

Q. Is that all, sir, you have ever seen him write? "a syllable or something" on your desk, which you do not remember?

A. I have seen him take the account of a cargo on the wharf.

Q. What sort of a cargo?

A. A cargo of iron and logwood.

Q. The account was kept by simply making a mark for each ton, was it not?

A. No, sir, *it is kept in figures.*

Q. Were you with him all the time, sir?

A. No, sir, I was not.

Q. How long were you with him?

A. I think he relieved me in a cargo in one of the instances where he weighed.

Question repeated.

A. I suppose for ten or fifteen minutes.

Q. Now, sir, do you say you saw him write on that occasion?

A. I saw him make the figures.

Q. Can he read writing?

A. I have never heard him.

Question repeated.

A. I have seen him pick up *a paper* addressed to *different ones* in the office, *and hand it to them.*

Q. Can he read writing? I want an answer to that question.

A. Well, I should say that was reading writing: further than that I do not know.

Q. Are you willing to swear that he can read writing? (*Mr. Brown objects to the question,* and it is overruled.)

Q. Are the returns which you make out verified by the oath of George Read?

A. Yes, sir.

Q. Is he capable of reading and understanding those returns?

A. He understands them, I don't know whether he can read them or not.

Q. If you don't know whether he can read them or not, how can you swear that he understands them?

A. He sees the business done every day that composes the account.

Question repeated.

Witness says he gives the same answer.

Q. How does he know that your account, is an exhibit of that daily work?

A. When I hand him the account *I generally tell him what month it is for.*

Q. Now, sir, is it the duty of the Weigher to oversee the accounts of his clerks?

A. They generally examine the *cash account.*

A. You have stated, sir, that it was his duty to oversee the whole department, and see that everything goes right?

A. I had reference to the business on the wharf when I stated that.

Q. Do you mean to say, sir, that it is not his duty to overlook the accounts of his department and see that they are right?

Q. I do not. *It is his duty certainly.*

Q. If such be his duty, and if you do not know whether he can read those accounts, or read the accounts which he verifies by his oath, how is it that you are willing to swear that he is a competent and efficient officer, as you have done? and the most efficient officer whom you have known?

A. He is always at his post, and I never knew but *one weigher that examined his accounts further than to know what the surplus and expenditure was.*

Q. Did you ever know a person to occupy that post before who could neither read nor write?

A. Not to my knowledge.

Q. You have said you always found him at his post, where is his post?

A. His post is on the wharf, sir, overseeing the laboring department.

Q. You have stated that vouchers for the expenditures of the department accompany your quarterly abstracts. What vouchers accompany those abstracts for the disbursements for daily or transient labor?

A. The wharf-book, in which the daily time of the men is kept; that is handed to the Deputy Collector and he vouches it, examines it.

Q. Now, sir, is there any other voucher for those payments *than your oath?*

A. No, sir! Those payments amount to some *six or seven thousand dollars a year, which are vouched only by my oath.*

It will be observed that much of the foregoing testimony, and parts of it which most strongly support the charge against Mr. Lewis, came from his own witnesses, not because they were willing to *admit the truth*, but only because they were *unable to conceal it.* And what does it establish? That the Weigh-master of the Port of Philadelphia can neither read nor write more than his own name; that he cannot spell the name of any vessel which may enter the Port; that he is unable to estimate the annual expenses of his Department, at a given rate per month; that all the accounts and abstracts from his office which the law requires to be verified by his oath, are sworn to by him, although he is utterly incapable of understanding a single item which they contain; and that from six thousand to seven thousand dollars of the public moneys pass into his hands in the course of every year, for the disbursement of which the collector requires no written voucher, but simply and only the unsupported oath of Charles H. Fisler! What becomes of the declaration made by Mr. Lewis through his counsel, that the competency of this Weigh-master is "*abundantly proved!*"

But Mr. Brown says that "Read has exhibited testimonials of his entire competency and ability from merchants whose dealings led them into perfect familiarity with the office of Weigher, and who therefore were competent to decide upon the fidelity and efficiency of the incumbent." Who are those merchants? Mr. Lewis did not venture to call a solitary merchant or man of business to testify on this point. No person who has had occasion to require the services of the Weigh-master, has been produced or offered as a witness in the case. But in the face of all the overwhelming proof above presented, Mr. Lewis has been content to *discredit his own witnesses* by spreading upon the record a paper purporting to have been signed by several respectable mercantile houses, to the effect that they have always found "George Read to be a prompt, attentive and efficient officer." This is an important document, although it is not evidence for Mr. Lewis; it is the same which he forwarded to the Department, in his letter to the Secretary of the Treasury of the 14th of November, *an act which proves him to be utterly unworthy of the confidence of the President, and of the position which he holds*, as a few words will be sufficient to show.

I am not informed how, or by whom the names to that paper were obtained, or whether they are genuine; but I am certain that no person who signed it, ever understood its object, or ever intended it as an expression of his deliberate, *intelligent* judgment. It is a daily event for men to sign their names to petitions, and recommendations for office, without reflection, and in the hurry of business, to oblige a friend, or to get rid of a troublesome importuner; and it is common law that no responsibility is incurred by the act. This certificate of George Read's competency as a public officer, must be classed among such papers; for it is not to be presumed that any respectable gentleman who may have subscribed it, intended to certify to what is evidently untrue, or imagined for a moment that it was to be used for an unworthy and dishonorable purpose. But not so with Mr. Lewis. He sent the paper to the Department on the 14th of November last, and he manifestly designed it as an anodyne for the minds of the President and the Secretary of the Treasury, which were disturbed on this question of the competency of a public officer, for whose acts they were indirectly responsible. *He knew that it did not represent the truth.* So far as it endorsed the competency of Read, it was contradicted by Mr. Lewis's *personal knowledge of the facts and of the man*, a knowledge which not one of the signers possessed, and yet he palmed it upon the President and the Secretary without a word of explanation, and for the plain purpose of deceiving them. That paper is now offered as his apology for retaining Read in office, and he *seeks to cast the responsibility of his act upon the gentlemen whose names are subscribed to it.*

The second part of the first specification, refers to a matter of record, which is established by the production of the record itself. Mr. Brown has been compelled to confess, that *Mr. Lewis knew* of the charges there made and exhibited, *some six or seven years ago*, but adds by way of avoidance, that *he never believed them!* A few extracts from Read's testimony, which is found in the Journal of the House, already cited, will effectually dispose of the lame leg on which he relies. On the 18th of February, 1842, READ was called before the Committee of which Judge Sharswood was Chairman, and testified (in part,) as follows;

Q. Were you at Harrisburg during the winter of 1840?
A. I do not know whether I was or not, but think it very likely.
Q. Do you remember whether you were here, at or about the time of the passage of the resumption resolutions?
A. I think I was.
Q. Did you attend at Harrisburg at the request of any of the banks?
A. *No sir.*
Q. Were you requested, while at Harrisburg, to act in behalf of any of the banks?
A. *No sir.*
Q. Were you allowed, or did you receive any compensation for services rendered any of the banks?
A. *No sir.*

* * * * *

Q. Did you render any services, that session, for the United States Bank, or any other bank?
A. *No sir, I did not; if I had I should have wanted pay for my services.*

* * * * *

Q. Did you see any bank officers while you were here?
A. *I see William D. Lewis here at one time*, but can't recollect it was then or not.

The Committee recalled Read on the 10th of June, 1842, when he testified as follows, to wit:

* * * * *

Q. When you were here before, you stated that you were at Harrisburg in 1840, will you please to state on what business and at whose request?
A. *I came here on account of the resumption resolutions, and at the request of Mr. George W. South.*
Q. Did Mr. South state to you, at the time you were to come to Harrisburg, in behalf of what particular bank?
A. I do not know that he did. He might have said it was on behalf of the U. S. Bank.
Q. Did you not understand yourself that you were to act on behalf of the Bank of the U. S.?
A. *I believe I did.*
Q. Did you correspond with any person while you were at Harrisburg?
A. *I did with Mr. South.*
Q. Who did you get to write your letters for you?
A. Mr Fields, I think, wrote a few for me.

* * * * *

Q. Did you receive any money from Mr. South?
A. *Yes sir.*
Q. How much?
A. *A thousand dollars.*
Q. Did you receive that all at one time, or at different times?
A. *All at one time.*

Q. At what time?

A. I cannot tell, it was after the Legislature adjourned. It may have been three weeks or three months afterwards, I do not know.

* * * * *

Q. What were the means you used to earn the $1000?

A. I do not know that I did anything.

Q. Did you make any further claim on the Bank of the U. S.?

A. No sir, I made no further claim. I asked Mr. South what they were going to give me. He said he did not know; he went down to the bank and brought me a $1000, which I put in my pocket.

Q. Did you not have such letters written as would procure the most money?

A. I did.

* * * * *

Q. Was it not your course at that time to write letters to Philadelphia, that you had influence with great men, for the purpose of procuring money?

A. I think it might have been.

* * * * *

Q. Did you state to any person that your services in behalf of the United States Bank were equal to a note there?

A. I told Mr. South so.

Q. When you were asked that same question before, why did you not answer as you do now?

A. I do not recollect answering that question.

Q. Upon your former examination you were asked this question, "Did you render any services that session for the United States Bank, or any other bank?" to which you answered, "No, sir, I did not. If I had I should wanted pay for my services." How do you explain that answer?

A. If I had done any service, I should have wanted larger pay.

The Committee, in their Report which accompanies the testimony, make the following comments on the statements of this witness:

"George Read, late Treasurer of the County of Philadelphia, was also one of the paid agents of the Bank, although he does not seem to have been trusted with money by the others, in which undoubtedly they showed their discernment and discretion. When he first appeared before the committee, he denied most positively and unequivocally, that he had ever been employed by any bank, paid by any bank, or rendered any services for which he had ever made any claim, and of course, that he knew any thing at all about the object of inquiry before the committee. Read is an extremely illiterate man, being unable to read or write, except his own name. He was obliged therefore to conduct his correspondence through the medium of an amanuensis. He procured for this purpose the services of John W. Nesbit, a clerk under him in the Treasurer's office, then attending at Harrisburg, to settle some accounts with the Auditor General, and upon his leaving Harrisburg, had the assistance of William Field, a member of the House from Bucks. In the letters written by Nesbit, being simple, but at the same time remarkably accurate accounts of the proceedings of the two Houses, there was nothing to arrest the attention of an amanuensis, but in several of those written by Mr. Field, there evidently was.

It is to be lamented that this gentleman's memory also failed him on this occasion, so that he was unable to recollect whether he had asked or received any explanation. And even in reference to a small note among the papers produced, addressed to him by Mr. Read, and urging him to come up, and attend to his business, 'or it would be all no go,' he could not remember to what it referred, so as to explain it. Mr. Field was often surprised at the information possessed by Read, and asked from what source he had obtained it, but received no satisfactory answer. The letters indeed do show that he was kept very well advised of what was doing and contemplated to be done.

Mr. South's letters, accompanying Read's show that Read received $1,000 for his services, and claimed to have a note of his for $1,000, held by the bank, delivered up. Mr. South, in his testimony, fails to explain his letters, at least to the satisfaction of the committee.

He testifies to the receipt of $1,600 from Mr. Handy, and that he paid Mr. Read only $1,000. Upon the bank threatening to sue him upon his note, Read intimated an intention to take defence, and call South as a witness; whereupon, rather than be called to testify in the case, Mr. South agreed to pay one-half the note, and accordingly did so, with or out of the $600 he had in hand. Mr. South has not explained satisfactorily, those remarkable expressions contained in his letter of the 17th April. 'Yesterday Mr. Read requested me to attend to his matters in relation to the late operations at Harrisburg. The Legislature having adjourned, he expects one or two individuals down who hold his engagements; I paid his order on me for $200, on Monday last; it is always better to settle with these persons at once, then their services can be again commanded when required.'

Upon his second appearance before the committee, Read admitted what he had before denied, that he knew that he was employed for the Bank of the United States—that he had received $1,000 for his services, and had claimed as a further compensation that his note for $1,000 should be given up. He explained his letters by the bold and unblushing assertion, that they were all mere fabrications, intended for the purpose of extorting money from the Bank. This witness then is self-convicted of fraud and perjury.

In regard to these three men, it must befor the constituted authorities to determine what the public justice of the country demands."

The testimony of Read, and the Report of the Legislative Committee have been before the eyes of Mr. Lewis ever since the year 1842. It is probable that no man who has his wits about him can scan the foregoing extracts from Read's testimony, and afterwards doubt the fact stated in the report of the committee, that he is self-convicted of corruption and perjury. Mr. Brown says, "*It is true*, that *Mr. Lewis knew of the charges against Read as asserted by the complainants, some six or seven years ago, but he never believed them!*" This *admission* establishes the second part of the first specification. Mr. Lewis' belief or his disbelief has nothing to do with the case, although he is probably the only person in Pennsylvania who would *profess* to entertain a doubt on the subject.

One excuse alleged by Mr. Brown for the appointment of Read, is that he was *repeatedly and urgently recommended by Mr. Cooper and his friends.* This is a matter of little importance, even if it were true. If the evidence is to be our guide in the settlement of such a question, Mr. Lewis has himself furnished all that is required to disprove the assertion of his Counsel. The testimony of George W. South, the same individual who is distinguished in the Report of the Legislative Committee, will perhaps satisfy an unbiassed judgment, that Mr. Lewis cannot shift the responsibility of Read's appointment from his own shoulders, which are so well suited to the burthen. Mr. South says that Mr. Cooper wrote two letters to Mr. Lewis, which passed through his hands, both bearing the same date, in which he recommended Geo. Read for the office of Weigh-master, and some other persons for other places. He also testified as follows: to wit,

Q. Did you and the other friends of Mr. Read obtain the approval of the authorities at Washington by anticipation before Mr. Lewis would make the appointment?

A. On the Thursday or Friday before Mr. Read's appointment, I was in the City, and called to see Mr. Lewis at the Custom House, to ascertain, if possible, if he intended Mr. Read to that post or not. I found Mr. Lewis in a little different mood from a few days before. He rather faltered upon the subject of appointing Mr. Read, for I supposed he was going to throw him overboard. I inquired the cause of his changing his mind. He said the *Ultra Whig party* had made a dead set at him, that he, Read, *had formerly been a Democrat.* Mr. Lewis added that *he had every disposition to accommodate Mr. Cooper and myself.* I went home to the country feeling very uncertain as to whether Read would be appointed or not.

On Sunday morning I received a message from Philadelphia, stating that Mr. David Winebrener and George J. Weaver, desired particularly to see me upon that subject. I came to town immediately, and saw Mr. Winebrener and Mr. W.

Q. Did Mr. Lewis agree to appoint him until after you should apply to the authorities at Washington?

A. *No, sir.*

Q. Did you so apply?

A. *Yes, sir, we did.*

Q. Was the appointment by anticipation?

A. *It was by the Sec. of the Treas'y, Mr. Meredith.*

Q. Was this approval communicated to Mr. Lewis?

A. *It was.*

Q. Was he afterwards appointed?

A. *He was.*

* * * * * * *

Being cross-examined, the witness further testified on this point as follows, to wit:

Q. At whose request did you visit the Sec. of the Treas'y in relation to Read's appointment?

A. I understood it to be at Mr. Lewis' request.
Q. Who called upon Mr. Meredith with you?
A. Mr. David Winebrener, Mr. George Weaver.
Q. Was Mr. Levin with you?
A. No, sir, not on that occasion.
Q. Did he accompany you at any visit to any functionary in Washington, in relation to Read's appointment?
A. Mr. Levin accompanied Mr. Weaver, Mr. Winebrenner, Mr. Dall and myself on a visit to Mr. Clayton, to the Sec. of War, Mr. Crawford, Mr. Preston, in relation to the appointment of Geo. Read. *Mr. Levin spoke of him, and it was to advise his appointment. He was appointed immediately on our return, which was a day or two after.*
Q. Why, sir, was it deemed necessary that the consent of Mr. Meredith to the appointment of Read should be had before the appointment was made?
A. *Mr. Lewis said that clamors had been raised as to Read's politics,* and he did not wish to send his name down *until he knew whether Mr. Meredith would confirm it or not.*

* * * * *

Q. Did Mr. Cooper take any other part in this matter than to write the two letters which you have before spoken of?
A. *Never to my knowledge.*

Thus it is proved that Mr. Cooper, to oblige somebody, (perhaps Mr. South), wrote two letters to Mr. Lewis, both dated May 10, 1849, recommending the appointment of Read, together with some other persons. These letters were placed in the hands of South, and were by him sent to Mr. Lewis,—South swears that *Mr. Cooper never took any other part in the matter.* He also proves that Mr. Lewis and himself were *more anxious than any other persons that Read should have the office of Weigh-master.* It was at *the request of Mr. Lewis* that South, Winebrenner, and Weaver visited Washington to obtain the assent of the authorities there, to Read's appointment. In company with Mr. Lewis C. Levin, they visited Mr. Meredith, Mr. Crawford, Mr. Clayton, and Mr. Preston, *to obtain their consent,* and Read "was appointed immediately on our return," says Mr. South, "which was a day or two afterwards." Why did Mr. Lewis move so cautiously in this matter? Why did he resort to the unusual expedient of *sending a committee to different members of General Taylor's cabinet,* to obtain from them a recommendation of Read's appointment? *This is the only instance of the kind which occurred in all the appointments which he made!* There is an attempt to explain it by the allegation that "the *ultra* Whig party" was opposed to Read because he had *formerly* been a Democrat! Hence, Mr. Lewis desired to throw the responsibility of the act upon the cabinet! If

Mr. Lewis had always entertained such a profound respect for the wishes of the "ultra Whigs," perhaps there might have been some excuse for a Cabinet Council to determine the momentous question, whether an apostate Democrat should be Weigh-master of the Port of Philadelphia? But, unluckily for him, and for his argument, he has appointed Democrats to office, and has retained Democrats in office, and has not considered it necessary to despatch committees on similar errands in such cases, either from fear or affection for the "ultra Whig party." In Johnston Kelley's letter to General Shields, dated Aug. 1, 1850, which was suggested and afterwards revised and approved by Mr. Lewis himself, and was therefore in fact his own production, the General is strongly urged to vote for his confirmation, on the ground that he was opposed by "*the bigots*;" (whether the epithet was intended for the Whigs or the Natives, or for both, does not appear) and on the further ground that "*no good could ensue to the Democratic party* by his rejection, and *much injury might thereby be inflicted on the numerous Democrats he has retained in office.*" This sufficiently exhibits his regard for the "ultra Whig party," and compels me to seek a better explanation than Mr. South has given of his object in sending his Committee to Washington.

Such an explanation is not difficult. By reference to the testimony of Mr. Lewis before the Committee of the Legislature, to be found in the Journal which accompanies the record in this case, the following remarkable passages may be read, to wit:

Q. Did you ever receive from the bank of the United States, or any of its officers or agents, any money for being employed at Harrisburg for their benefit?

A. Not a dollar.

* * * * * * * *

Q. Among the vouchers of the permanent expenses of the Bank of the United States there is one for seven thousand five hundred dollars, and is a receipt of Mr. Biddle, *with your name endorsed on the back of it in pencil*—have you any knowledge of it?

A. I have no knowledge of it; and at the time this voucher was published in the Philadelphia papers, I endeavored to ascertain from *my own cash book* whether such a sum had been received by me, *but it did not appear to have been received.*

Q. Did the Girard Bank, of which you are Cashier, contribute anything towards the passage of the resumption resolutions in 1840, in the shape of money?

A. No, sir, it did not.

Q. Do you know of any means having been employed directly or indirectly, by any of the Banks at any time, for the purpose of procuring any legislation for their benefit?

A. I do not.

* * * * * * *

Q. Did you ever get at that time, (1836,) or at *any time,* money from Mr. George Handy, in connection with disbursements for the Bank of the United States?

A. No, sir.

The testimony of *Mr. Alexander Lardner,* who had been the Cashier of the Bank of the United States, will be found in the same Journal. He proves that a special Committee of which Mr. Handy was the principal acting member, was appointed by the Bank on the 3d of March, 1840, to proceed to Harrisburg, and take charge of the interests of the Bank during the Session of the Legislature. The following questions and answers will be found in his testimony.

Q. Do you remember or know of any voucher endorsed by William D. Lewis, for seven thousand three hundred dollars?

A. I do not: *I know of the sum of three thousand and some odd hnndred dollars passed to the credit or paid on the check of Wm. D. Lewis, by order of this Special Committee of March* 3, 1840. I do not know for what purpose.

* * * * *

Q. Do you know of the payment of $1000 to Mr. George W. South, by this Committee?

A. I only know it from the face of the voucher; that order may have been paid by me, but I have no recollection of it now, nor do I know the object for which it was paid.

The money paid to and expended by the Special Committee during the session of the Legislature, was upwards of *one hundred and thirty thousand dollars.* The examination of Mr. Handy will be found in the Journal, in which the following question and answer occur:

Q. When you paid this large amount of money, did you not know that you were paying it for corrupt purposes?

A. I can't deny it.

Mr. Handy proved that *Geo. W. South was one of the agents of the Bank, and received part of the money,* and Mr. Lardner proves that three thousand some odd hundred dollars of it passed to the credit, or was paid on the check of *Wm. D. Lewis.* It has already been seen, that Read was also employed as one of the agents of the Bank, *at the instance of South.*

Turning again to the testimony of Mr. George W. South, in this case, we find at the close of it the following remarkable passages.

Q. Mr. South, you were acquainted with Mr. Lewis during those Bank operations at Harrisburg, were you not?

A. I was, sir.

Q. You acted together there, representing pretty nearly the same parties?

A. No, sir, I was not there. We did not act together *there*, or represent the same parties. *I had nothing to do with it!*

Q. Did you not employ George Read?

The witness declines answering.

The answer is insisted upon. *Mr. Brown objects*, and *the question is overruled.*

Honest Mr. South!

We have now the explanation of Read's appointment to the office of Weigh-master. Mr. Lewis knew the man, and his character. He had made his acquaintance when the banks required legislative aid, and sought to obtain it by bribery and corruption; and Read knew both Mr. Lewis and Mr. South. He knew the secrets which a legislative investigation had failed to extract from the oblivious memories of his friends and patrons, and he wanted office. A feeling stronger than mere gratitude, one which sprang from a close fellowship in transactions, from which the feeblest ray of light might start a thousand sources of disgrace, quickened the ingenuity of Mr. Lewis and Mr. South, to satisfy the *demand* of their ancient confrere and confederate.

It required some ingenuity; for how could the object be accomplished in a way to relieve Mr. Lewis from the indignation which a virtuous community might manifest, when it should be announced that a man who could neither read nor write, and who stood self-convicted of perjury and corruption on the legislative records of Pennsylvania, was appointed to the responsible post of Weigh-master of the Port of Philadelphia? Mr. South discloses the plan which was adopted. He and his Committee were despatched to Washington; they waited upon the members of General Taylor's Cabinet, and Mr. Lewis C. Levin, as their foreman, *advised that the Collector of the Port should be requested to make the appointment.* The Cabinet officers, doubtless, uninformed as to the character of the individual, and, as doubtless deceived as to his capacity for the post, yielded to the persuasive eloquence of Mr. Levin: the Committee returned to Philadelphia, the Weigh-master was forthwith commissioned, the endangered secrets were preserved, and Mr. Lewis, innocent, unsuspecting, virtuous man, now washes his hands of all responsibility!

It has now been proved, that "the Collector of the Port of Philadelphia is guilty of a want of fidelity to the Government, and to the character of the present administration, by *retaining in the office of Weigh-master* a person whom he has always known to be incompetent for the proper performance of the duties of the said office, and who stands charged with perjury on the legislative records of Pennsylvania, a fact well known to the Collector at the time that he appointed him to the said office?" And this disposes of the first specification.

I come now to the second specification.

The Collector and Surveyor of the Port of Philadelphia were instrumental in procuring fictitious signatures to certain printed letters, addressed to members of the Senate of the United States, urging the confirmation of the said Collector, whose name was then before the Senate, and that said signatures were obtained through the Weigh-master, acting in the matter with their knowledge and consent, and that said letters were forwarded as genuine letters to certain Senators by the said Collector and Surveyor of the Port of Philadelphia."

The first point to be determined by the evidence is, were fictitious names signed to such papers? This fact is established by the production of some of the papers themselves, which had been forwarded to members of the Senate, and which are now attached to the record of these proceedings, marked to which I beg leave to refer. The evidence of this fact is so overwhelming, that Mr. Brown is compelled to admit it: but he alleges that neither Read nor Fisler had any participation in the matter, and that Mr. Lewis was utterly ignorant of the transaction. We shall see how far Mr. Brown's assertions are sustained by the evidence.

Mr. John E. Murray, one of the Deputy Weighers, and a very *unwilling witness* against his employer, was asked,

"Do you know of any person who wrote any other name than his own to any of those circulars in the Weigher's office?"

(*Question objected to by Mr. Brown.* Objection overruled.)

A. I do, sir.

Q. Who was that person?

(*Objected to by Mr. Brown, and the Commissioner decides that it must be restricted to persons in the Custom House.*)

Q. Did you sign any names to any of those circulars other than your own, and if so, at whose request?

(Mr. Brown requests the Commissioner to instruct the witness *that he is not bound to answer the question.* The Commissioner instructs the witness that he is not bound to state any fact which would implicate himself: but if the witness can state that he subscribed the names of others, *by authority from them,* he is bound to do so.)

A. I don't see how I can answer that question direct. I have signed names—two or three names at the farthest. It might have been on two or three circulars, at the request of Mr. Read, Weigh-master.

Q. State the circumstances of the transaction.

A. I was in the office at noon, making my book, and there was several persons in the office, Mr. Read, Mr. Fisler, Mr. Brady, Mr. Zane and myself. The printed circulars spoken of were handed out, I think, by Mr. Read, and it is my belief that names were added to those papers. Mr. Read asked me to write some names, and gave me the names of two or three persons at the farthest, of persons who were willing to have their names appended. Those persons were not present. I wrote their names.

* * * * *

Q. Who told you that the persons whose names you wrote desired to have them written on the circulars?

A. *Mr. Read, the Weigh-master.*

Q. Did Mr. Read ask any other persons to sign names in your presence?

A. I think he did.

Q. Whom did he ask?

A. I don't remember who, but it was one of the gentlemen in the office—I mean some one of the officers.

Q. What did Read say when he took the circulars out, and what did he do?

A. Well, I cannot remember the language he made use of at the time, the idea was, they were handed out to have names appended, but anything about the language I can't tell—I can't remember.

Q. Did you see him hand them out for signature by the men in the office on more than one occasion?

A. I believe I did.

Q. How often?

A. Well, on two or three occasions.

Q. Do you know whether names were signed on those occasions?

A. That is my impression.

MR. JOEL ZANE, a deputy weigher, testifies as follows:—

Q. After every exertion had been made by those in the office to obtain signatures, the plan of obtaining the fictitious names was then adopted by Mr. Read. Some days there would be enough papers in the office containing genuine signatures to supply the number he said he required to take to the Custom House. At other times it would require one, sometimes two, and sometimes three circulars to make up the deficiency. He would then take from his desk the number required, and hand them to whoever would be in the office at that time, requesting them to fill them up with ten but not more than twelve names. After being filled up he would take all the papers, genuine and fictitious, and say he must take them to the Custom House, as Mr. Norris wished so many papers on that day.

Q. State in what manner they were filled up with names, and what directions were given by George Read, and what acts were done by him to that end?

A. The papers were filled alternately by those in the office, that is, names were signed to them, papers being handed to each person by Mr. Read for that purpose; different kinds of pens were used, and different kinds of ink, both blue and black; very often after being filled up they would be handed to some one in the office for the purpose of having the Congressional District from which they came, inserted.

Q. How long was this matter in progress?

A. As near as I can recollect, a month or six weeks.

Q. Were there many of these filled up with fictitious names in your office?

A. There was. I cannot give any idea as to the number, sometimes a week would elapse, and sometimes two or three days and none would be signed, and some might have been signed when I was not in the office. It occurred previous to the confirmation of Mr. Lewis.

Q. Who of the Deputy Weighers were principally concerned in signing those names?

A. Mr. Fisler, Mr. Brady and myself.

Q. How were the names which you signed procured?

A. There was no regular mode that I am aware of, except one occasion, when a city directory was handed to Mr. Brady, he was ordered by Mr. Read to take the names from that.

Q. Do you know whether Mr. Brady took any names from it?

A. I do not.

Q. Were the names which were signed those of living persons?

A. They were not to my knowledge, but were fictitious.

Q. What induced you to sign those names?

A. The threats of Mr. George Read, that no person friendly to the confirmation of Mr. Lewis, would refuse to do so, and that if we did refuse, we would be removed from office.

Read also placed a number of the circulars in the hands of Charles Knecht, a clerk in Alberger's store, which was at that time near the weigher's office. They were filled by Knecht principally, who returned them to Read as they were called for. With every disposition to conceal his principal in the fraud, Knecht testifies as follows, to wit:—

Q. Did you ever see either of those papers before?

A. I think I have seen paper marked "A.A.," the other I have not seen to my knowledge.

Q. Where did you see that paper?

A. I saw it at our counting house.

Q. By whom was it placed there?

A. It was given to me by Mr. Geo. Read.

Q. For what purpose?

A. For the purpose of getting signatures attached to it.

Q. Did he give it to you unsigned?

A. Yes.

Q. Who signed those names to it?

A. I signed them pretty much, nearly all myself, sir.

Q. At whose request?

A. At the request of the parties whose names they call for, principally.

Q. Name the parties whose names you signed at their request, and their residence.

A. Here is James Sullivan, *I am not aware where he lives, sir*. He is a boy who called at the office, and I signed his name at his request. Charles Durfer, he was a butcher's apprentice, who came to the office at that time to collect a small bill; I don't know where he resides. *They are principally all of the same kind.* Robert Snyder, he is a boy who also called at the office, I don't know his residence or anything further about him. Elijah Wheaton, he is a person who at that time kept a tavern at the corner of Broad and Turner's Lane; he has since gone to California, so I have been told, at least. William Myers, he is another butcher's boy, I don't know where he lives. These are all the names I signed to it: my own is not there.

Q. Who signed the first name, Thompson McDonough?

A. I don't know. I did not see any body write it, and don't know who did it. I don't know such a person as Thompson McDonough.

Q. Who signed the name of Robert Garrigan?

A. I don't know, sir.

Q. Who signed the name of J. Howard Wakely?

A. I don't know, sir; I don't know such a person.

Q. Who signed the name of Jacob T. Troutt?

A. An individual who called at the store, and I requested him to sign his name. He put down that name; whether that was his name or not, I am unable to say.

* * * * *

Q. Who wrote the name of Samuel Hallowell?

A. That I added myself to complete the list. It is fictitious; there is no such person to my knowledge.

Q. Why did you write all these names in a different hand?

A. To give them a better appearance—to make them appear as if they had been written by different parties.

Q. When you completed the signatures of these names, to whom did you give this paper?

A. I handed it Mr. George Read, from whom I had received it.

Q. There were other papers signed in the same way, were there not?

A. Yes, there might have been five or six.

Q. Were they all given to Mr. George Read?

A. Yes, sir.

Mr. George T. Thorn, an Inspector of the Customs, was also applied to by Read, to fill one or more of the circulars with fictitious or forged names. He testifies as follows:

A. I entered the weigher's office one day upon some business, the character of which I do not remember, it was in connection with my duties, however. Mr. Read was sitting at a desk. After transacting the business that called me to his office, Mr. Read handed me two or three copies of this circular, and requested me to get them signed. I took the circulars from him and retained them in my possession some days. Mr. Read came to the end of a wharf where I was employed, a few days subsequent to the one in which he gave me the circulars, and asked me if I had got them signed. I told him I had not. He asked me, why; I told him I did not think it prudent for an officer of the customs to be conveying such petitions through the city, that I thought the circulation of such petitions promiscuously, was calculated to do Mr. Lewis more injury than good, that if they were shown to a person an enemy of Mr. Lewis', it would be immediately known at Washington, and the officers would be charged with neglecting their duty to procure signatures for the confirmation of the Collector. Mr. Read replied that I was a fool, that he had got a great many of them signed himself, and thought they would do a great deal of good. He then asked me to get some friend to have it filled if I would not do it myself; I replied I would do so. A day or two afterwards, I don't exactly remember how long it was, I met Mr. Read again, he asked me if I had got signatures to the circular; I told him I had not; he said I was a great while about it, or something to that effect, and told me *I could fill it up myself and hand it to him,* which of course I objected to do. He then told me, if I would not hand *it to him, to take it to Mr. Norris.* I told him that if I got the circular filled, I would send it to Washington myself; he replied that all that had been filled had been sent away, I think he said from the Custom House, and stated that there was *some system employed in sending them away,* that he or they (I do not know which was used) did not want too many sent to *the same senator,* was the reason he gave why I should hand it to him. There was some other conversation, but this was substantially all that was said at the concluding interview.

Q. When he told you, you could fill up the circulars yourself, what did you say to him in reply?

A. I told him he had mistaken his man, I could not be guilty of such an act.

Q. Did he make any reply to that remark?

A. I do not remember what was said in reply by Mr. Read.

Q. Were the relations then existing between Mr. Lewis, Mr. Norris, and George Read intimate and confidential or otherwise? (*Objected to by Mr. Brown, and question overruled in that form.*)

Q. State your knowledge of the connection, and relations then existing between Mr. Lewis, Mr. Norris, and Mr. Read.

(*Objected to by Mr. Brown, and question overruled.*)

Q. Have you or have you not known Mr. Lewis, George Read, and Mr. Norris to be closeted in the Custom House repeatedly during the circulation of the circulars in question, and do you or not know that Read was acting in the matter with the knowledge and consent of the other persons named. (*Objected to by Mr. Brown, and first part of the question overruled,* and under the decision of the Commissioner, Mr. Gibbons declines the further examination of the witness.)

Mr. Francis E. Brady, in reference to the names signed in the Weigher's office to the circulars, testified as follows:

A. George Read took them out of his desk and told me to sign names to those blank petitions; I refused, and stated at the time, that the Senate of the United States were a body of men who could not be imposed on by fictitious names signed to those papers. Mr. Fisler was present and Mr. Zane. I am not certain whether Murray was present or not. Mr. Fisler resisted signing names as well as myself. Read swore violently and said, *none but enemies of Mr. Lewis would refuse to sign them.* We all, Fisler, Zane, Murray, and myself, all signed alternately, Murray only signed upon two occasions, how many names he signed each time I don't know. After we had signed and filled the paper with ten or twelve names, (I think it was twelve that Read requested to have on the paper) we handed the paper to the Weigh-master, finished. He rubbed it between his hands and threw it on the floor. After he had rubbed the paper and threw it on the floor, he picked it up and smoothed it out again, and put it in his desk: he done this on several occasions. Others were filled up in the same way, and *taken to the Custom House by Read.* I have heard Read repeatedly say that *he had taken them to the Custom House.*

Q. How many papers were filled up in the office in this way?

A. It is impossible for me to tell the numbers. We signed from the commencement of July until some time towards the middle of August, I think, at intervals: some days we would sign none, and at other times we would finish four or five papers in one day, *just as Mr. Read would order them.*

Q. In what way would he order them?

A. He would say *I want four or five of those papers filled for Mr. Norris to forward to Washington,* then we would fill the papers as desired by him. They were then taken by George Read to the Custom House, so he stated. Mr. Read stood between us—Fisler, Zane, and myself—there were two desks on each side of the office and he handed the paper alternately to us, after I had signed he would hand it to either Zane or Fisler, and proceed in that way until the paper was filled. He brought to the office as he stated, from the Custom House, a bundle of quills. We wrote with steel pens and quill pens. We had three inkstands, and *Mr. Read with water regulated the color of the ink to vary it.* Mr. Read was not always present when we signed; he would leave orders that when we came to the office at twelve o'clock, the usual hour for dinner, to fill up so many of the papers. The orders were left with myself on some occasions, and with Zane (as Zane told me) when I would come into the office.

* * * * * *

Q. Were the names which you signed genuine, and those of living persons, or otherwise? and how did you obtain them?

A. George Read handed me the Directory, and told me to take the names from that. I wrote names of persons, don't know whether living or dead. As the papers were marked for different districts, 1st, 2d, 3d, and 4th; Read wished names to correspond with the District. I refer now to the circulars forwarded from the office a short time previous to the confirmation of Mr. Lewis. I did not copy names from the Directory. Read was not able to tell whether I did or not, as he can neither read nor write, or spell the name of any vessel in the Port of Philadelphia.

* * * * * *

Q. Did any other person than Geo. Read take any of the papers from the Weigher's office after they had been signed in the manner you have mentioned?

A. I have no knowledge of any person carrying those papers away but Read.

Q. When did Read say that he took them to the Custom House?

A. Immediately after he had commenced signing those papers, and during the whole time those names were signed in the office, I understood from Mr. Read they were taken by him to the Custom House.

Q. Did he ever say to whom he gave them at the Custom House?

A. On one occasion he came back from the Custom House to the office very angry, and stated that a paper *badly signed* had been thrown out of the papers taken up *by Mr. Lewis.* This paper referred to, was signed at a Tavern, and by one person, *who was a bad writer.* That is the only instance that I recollect Mr. Lewis' name to have been mentioned in connection with those papers. He stated generally, as I have said, that *Mr. Norris wanted these papers to forward to Washington.*

This mass of testimony clearly establishes the participation of George Read, and Fisler his chief clerk, in the transactions to which the witnesses refer. Mr. Brown alleges it to be *untrue* that "Lewis and Read were on terms of the closest intimacy." Why, then, did he object to every question which was intended to prove such an intimacy? When Mr. Thorn was asked, "*Were the relations then existing between Mr. Lewis, Mr. Norris, and Geo. Read, intimate and confidential, or otherwise,*" why did Mr. Brown interpose and prevent an answer? When the same witness was requested to state *his knowledge of the connection and relations then existing between Lewis, Norris, and Read,* why did Mr. Brown again object, and suggest that *the inquiry was not pertinent to the issue?* When the same witness was again asked, "Have you or have you not known Lewis, Norris, and Read to be closeted in the Custom House repeatedly during the circulation of the circulars in question, and do you or do you not know that Mr. Read was acting in the manner with the knowledge and consent of the other persons named," why did Mr. Brown strenuously object to the question, if he believed what he asserts, that *no intimacy existed between them?*

But this intimacy is clearly and fully established by all the evidence in the case. The repeated declarations of Read, his daily visits to the Custom House, with the printed circulars filled with names fictitious and otherwise, his freedom in entering the Collector's private room on all occasions, his consultation with Lewis and Norris in the presence of Ellmaker, his presence at the caucus which was held on the subject of the fictitious signatures, at which Mr. M'Michael was present, with Lewis and Norris, and the *careful exclusion of every other officer except Fisler, connected with the Weigher's department*, his employment by Mr. Lewis to obtain letters from the deputies to Whig members of the Senate, in favor of his confirmation, *on the ground that he was a Whig*, and his agency in procuring the letter to Gen. Shields which was revised by Mr. Lewis himself, and signed by Johnston Kelly, beseeching his vote in favor of the confirmation on the ground that *his rejection would injure the Democratic party*, are all authenticated, stubborn facts, uncontradicted and unexplained, which carry with them absolute conviction that Lewis, Norris, and Read were on the most intimate and confidential terms. There is still another fact which tends strongly to the same conclusion. While Mr. Brown, as the counsel of Mr. Lewis, has labored hard to prove that his client is not responsible for Read's appointment, he warmly espouses the cause of Read himself, and under the overwhelming evidence which crushes him to the earth, cries out that Read is a competent man and suitable in all respects for the office which he holds. He so completely identifies the cause of Mr. Lewis with that of Read, that judgment against one is *necessarily* a condemnation of both.

But Mr. Brown in his "argument," relies on the testimony of South, Fisler, Johnston Kelly, and Benjamin Robinson, to annihilate that of all the other witnesses in the case. The credibility of South and Fisler may be judged of by the sample which I have already exhibited, and from the connection which exists between them and the principal parties. When South swore that Read was able to read the orders of the County Commissioners "when they were written very plainly," he knew better, as the construction of his answer clearly indicates. He well knew that he was not then acquainted with the letters of the Alphabet, and that on the day which he testified before the Commissioner, the school master was still abroad, and that his friend Read had never been introduced to that distinguished and useful citizen: when he deliberately swore at the close of his testimony that *he had nothing to do with the bank operations at Harrisburg, in* 1840, he exposed his readiness to swear to anything which might be necessary to the vindication of his friends

Lewis and Read without regard to the truth. It has been shown that he was a prominent actor in that nefarious proceeding, that he received money from the Bank, that Read was employed by him, that all the letters which Read caused to be written for the purpose of extorting money, were addressed to him, and passed through his hands, and yet he swears without hesitation, that he "*had nothing to do with it!*" His lively interest in his friend did not abate after he was made Weigh-master. Although he is a citizen of another county, and lives some fifteen miles from Philadelphia, it has ever been his custom to visit the Weigh-master, who can dispose of the public moneys without a voucher, sometimes once, sometimes twice, sometimes thrice in every week; visits of *friendship* he says, and not of business. And this Damon of Bucks county now comes, not to *die*, but to swear for Pythias!

Fisler is the next prominent witness for the defence. He is one of the principal parties implicated, and the same individual who "*swore the matter through*" before Mayor Jones; who makes up all of Read's accounts, and whose unsupported oath is *the only voucher* for the disbursement of between *six and seven thousand dollars of the public money which pass into the hands of Read, in the course of every year!* A few extracts from his testimony, in addition to what has been already given, will show the character of the evidence on which Mr. Brown rests his defence of Lewis and Read.

Q. By Mr. Brown. During the pendency of the confirmation of Mr. Lewis before the Senate, were you ever directed or requested by Mr. Read to sign as many names to certain circulars in regard to that pending question as you could, or to sign any names at all irregularly?

A. *I was not, sir.*

Q. To your knowledge, was any body in that office, ever so directed or requested by Mr. Read?

A. No, sir.

Q. Did you ever sign such names?

A. No, sir.

Q. As far as you know, sir, or saw, were there any fictitious names, that is names not authorized to be signed, I mean signed to those circulars by any body in that office?

A. I never *saw* any signed, sir.

Q. Did you ever request any of the weighers to swear the matter through before the Mayor?

A. No, sir.

On his cross-examination the following questions and objections will be found.

Q. When did you first hear of the fictitious signatures?

(Question objected to by Mr. Brown, and overruled by the Commissioner!)

Q. Had you no conversation with Mr. Murray, or Brady, or Zane about the investigation before the Mayor?

(Objected to by Mr. Brown and question overruled!)

* * * * *

Q. Now, sir, had you not at that very time large sums of money bet on Mr. Lewis' confirmation?

A. *I decline answering that question.*

Q. On what ground do you decline?

A. *On the ground of not criminating myself.*

The witness further testified that he made an affidavit on the subject *prior to the confirmation of Mr. Lewis, and at the request of Mr. Lewis*, and that he made a second affidavit *also at his request* after Brady's removal. *He delivered to Mr. Lewis both of these affidavits.* The original of one, and a copy of the other will be found attached to the return of the Commissioner, marked No. 19 and No. 20. The two affidavits give *different versions* of his alleged conversation with Mr. Brady in relation to Mr. Mc Grath's statements concerning the fictitious signatures. The attention of the witness was directed to the discrepancy, but he was *unable to explain it.* Two months elapsed between the dates of the affidavit, and when he was asked why he was more precise in the second than he had been in the first, he could only answer, "*I have no reason.*" His activity in preparing testimony for the defence, his equivocation on the subject, his declaration that he had written but *one* affidavit in relation to it, his subsequent admission that he had prepared a second, and finally a third, and all at the instance of Read, will sufficiently appear in the following additional extracts from his cross-examination.

Q. Pray, sir, did you prepare affidavits for other persons respecting this matter?

A. I did prepare an affidavit for Mr. Zane, *that is all.*

Q. Did he swear to it?

A. No, sir, he did not.

Q. What did you do with that?

A. *I destroyed it.*

Exhibit No. 16, handed witness.

Q. Is not that the affidavit you prepared for Zane?

A. No, sir, I never saw that before.

Q. Who requested you to prepare an affidavit for Zane?

A. *Mr. George Read asked me to get his affidavit.*

Q. Now, sir, you say you prepared no other affidavit?

A. Not to my recollection. I don't think I did. I think I did copy an affidavit. It was dictated to me by the person who made it.

Q. Who was that person?

A. Mr. Robinson. Mr. Benjamin Robinson.

Q. Did George Read tell you to get that affidavit, too?

A. I think he did, sir.

Q. Did you prepare no other for any other person?

A. Not to my recollection.

Q. Didn't you prepare or copy one for George Read himself?

A. I think I did copy one for him.

Q. Did he dictate it to you?

A. He did, sir, I think.

Q. Then, sir, you prepared it for him, did you not?

A. I wrote it as he dictated it.

Q. Did he swear to it immediately afterwards?

A. I don't know, sir.

Q. After you had prepared it, did you read it to him?

A. Yes, sir.

Q. Did you read this part of it to him: "But if *I were as illiterate as he would make me appear, for he asserts twice in his card that I can neither read nor write,* I should hardly have been considered fit to serve as I did without discredit between two or three years as Treasurer of the County of Philadelphia."

A. I have heard them words before, but really I can't say whether they was in the affidavit or not.

Q. Did you see that affidavit after he had sworn to it?

A. I did not, sir.

Benjamin Robinson, the third witness for Lewis and Read, is connected with the latter by marriage, and holds the important post of *Weigh-master's messenger.* He made the following statements on his cross-examination:

Q. Who appointed you to office?

A. Mr. Read, sir.

Q. He created the office of messenger, did he not?

A. I can't say as to that, sir, whether he did or did not?

Q. Are you related to him?

A. Well, somewhat, through marriage.

Q. How?

A. My son married his sister.

Q. How long was the signing of names in the office, to the circulars you have mentioned, continued?

A. I never saw but the one day that they were filled in that way.

Q. Do you mean to say, sir, that it was never done on any other occasion?

A. Not to my knowledge.

Q. Did you ever converse with Mr. Read on the subject?

A. I did not, sir.

Q. Did you ever make an affidavit on this subject?

A. I did, sir.

Q. At whose request?

A. Mr. Fisler's.

Q. Did you never see Mr. Fisler sign any names?

A. To my knowledge, sir, I never did.

Q. I scarcely understand your answer; do you mean to say that you do not remember whether he did it or did not, or that he did not do it, which?

A. I don't remember seeing him do it.

Q. Do you remember signing a name or two yourself?

A. I remember signing my own name.

Q. Any other name?

A. Not that I recollect of.

Q. Do you remember on any occasion saying in the office, in reference to the signing of fictitious names, when will this business be done, or something to that effect?

A. I do not remember any such words, or anything to that effect?

Q. Did you consider the filling up of those papers in the office at the time you have mentioned to be an improper act?

A. Well, I didn't think it was the proper thing.

Q. Then, how happens it, sir, that you never mentioned it to your employer?

A. I didn't wish to have any ill-will about the office with any of them.

Q. To whom did you first communicate it?

A. To Mr. Fisler.

Q. When?

A. About two months ago, as nearly as I can tell.

Q. Before or after Brady's card was published?

A. That, sir, I can't answer, for I don't know when it was published.

Q. Was it before or after his removal from office?

A. I think it was before he was removed, sir.

Q. How long before?

A. I can't exactly tell, it was a short time before.

Q. You have just said, sir, that you did not communicate it to Geo. Read, because you did not wish the ill-will of those in the office, how happens it that you mentioned it to Fisler?

A. Mr. Fisler asked me about it, sir, and that was before Brady's removal.

Q. Was it before Mr. Lewis' confirmation?

A. No, sir, I think Mr. Lewis was confirmed at that present time.

Q. Did Mr. Fisler tell you why he asked you?

A. Well, he said there was something going on in that department that he didn't think was quite right, and he wished to know what I knew about the fictitious signatures.

Q. Did he tell you that he wanted you to make an affidavit?

A. He did, sir.

Q. Did he write the affidavit at that time?

A. He did, sir.

Q. Mr. Brady was removed in October; you have stated that this conversation was prior to Brady's removal, and that Fisler wrote the affidavit at that time; how happens it that you did not swear to the affidavit until the 23d November?

A. I swore to it as soon as I got it.

Q. What part of the day, sir, were you absent from the Weigher's office?

A. Sometimes I was absent in the morning, sometimes in the afternoon, sometimes half a dozen times through the day.

* * * * * * *

Q. Did your duties as messenger, or otherwise, frequently take you away from the office?

A. Some days they called me away the best part of it, other days I was there pretty much all the time.

Q. You state in this affidavit, sir, *that you frequently saw Brady and Zane signing names to such papers,* and you have stated on your examination here, that you *never saw them do it but the once,* and to two circulars only, how do you reconcile this contradiction?

A. That is fictitious, I have seen them sign their own names to papers *extra of that?*

Q. Do you mean, sir, that you have seen them sign their own names frequently to those papers?

A. Oh no, sir.

Q. Do you mean that you saw them signing fictitious names frequently?

A. No, sir.

Q. What do you mean? explain this contradiction, if you can?

A. Why, I see them once sign fictitious names to papers, and I see them once sign their own names.

Q. Is that the only explanation that you desire to make?

A. Yes, sir.

It will be observed from the testimony of this witness, that after the confirmation of Mr. Lewis, and prior to the removal of Brady, and at a time when all was quiet on the subject of the fictitious signatures, Fisler informed the witness "that something was going on in the Weigher's Department which was not quite right," and asked him, "*what he knew about the fictitious signatures?*" He then prepared an affidavit for the witness, which he retained in his possession until the 23d of November, when he called upon Robinson to swear to it, which he accordingly did. The affidavit will be found annexed to the testimony, and contains the following clause, to wit;

"During the time which Mr. Wm. D. Lewis was before the Senate of the U. S. for confirmation as Collector, I have frequently seen Mr. George Read give Francis E. Brady and Joel Zane, circulars to be sent to U. S. Senators, with instructions to get as many signatures as they could to them. I *never heard Mr. Read give either of these gentlemen orders to sign any papers themselves,* but I have *frequently* seen them signing names to such papers during the absence of Mr. Read from the office. I have never seen any other person in the office sign these papers."

The affidavit, it will be remembered, was written by Fisler, as he states, at the request of George Read, *before* Mr. Brady was discharged, and Robinson was prepared to swear to it on demand. This strange proceeding was not without an object. It occurred at "a period of profound peace;" and we must not lose sight of the fact which will be found in South's testimony, that South, and Read, and Lewis, were in constant communication with each other on the subject of the fraud, about the same time. The removal of Mr. Brady was then in contemplation, but it was evidently deemed inexpedient to carry it into effect, until they were fully prepared to overwhelm him with affidavits, and swear him down, in case he should make a public exposure of the affair. This accounts for the activity of Read and Fisler in obtaining affidavits, in anticipation of the event, and Mr. Lewis lets the animal "out of the bag," in his letter to the Secretary of the Treasury, of the 14th November, wherein the following passage may be found:

"I removed him, (Brady,) *expecting*, nay threatened with the publication of just such a card as he has given to the world, *but feeling no apprehension of its injuring me.*" He evidently supposed, that through the agency of South, Read, and Fisler, he was provided with abundant ammunition for a successful defence, and would be able to overcome truth by falsehood, and satisfy the world that he was an innocent, persecuted man. It now appears, however, that Benjamin Robinson was not well trained by Fisler. In his affidavit, he swears positively that he saw Brady and Zane signing names to the papers, *frequently*, in the absence of Read; and before the Commissioner, he as positively swore that, he never saw them do it but once.

Johnston Kelly, the only other witness produced by Mr. Lewis, is a laborer in the Weigher's department, proves that he was put into condition and trained as a witness by Geo. W. South, and Lewis C. Levin. This is the same person whom Mr. Lewis used to secure the vote of Gen. Shields, supposing that the General would be willing to do him the slight favor which he asked, because he was born in the same part of Ireland from which the General himself came, a fact particularly set forth in the letter referred to, which accompanies the testimony. Some time in November last, Kelly found himself at the house of Mr. Levin, in conversation with that gentleman on the subject of Brady's card, but he has no recollection of the particulars of what was said. Soon after he found himself closeted with Mr. Geo. W. South, at the Weigher's office. "I saw Mr.

South *up-stairs* in the office," says Kelly, "and he wrote me a copy of an affidavit concerning Mr. Brady, and Mr. Zane—*what they said to me—that's all.*

Q. Did you make the affidavit?
A. Yes, sir.
Q. What was done with it?
A. I can't say, it went out of my hands.
Q. Who took it?
A. *I left it at Mr. Levin's.*

* * * * * * *

(The affidavit was called for but could not be produced.)
Q. Who first asked you to make that affidavit?
A. *Mr. Levin, sir.*
Q. Was it part of your affidavit that this matter was a conspiracy?
A. No. *I told Mr. South it was, but that wasn't put in the affidavit!*

Such are the witnesses upon whom Mr. Lewis relies, to carry him and his friend George Read safely through this investigation. They have been banded together from the very start of the fraud. South's credibility is utterly destroyed by his prevarication and his falsehood, apparent upon the face of his testimony; to say nothing of his association and connection with the principal parties, and his activity in preparing evidence on their behalf, which tend strongly to impeach his integrity. Fisler is directly implicated in the fraud: he is one of the instruments always in order to be used for any purpose which his master may require; and he and Robinson, and Kelly, are secure in their respective positions, only so long as Lewis and Read are continued in office. Hence they have such a direct and certain interest in the result, as would in ordinary cases exclude them as witnesses. But in addition to this, their testimony, like that of South, carries with it the evidence of insincerity and corruption.

I beg leave now to introduce some of the material parts of the deposition of Mr. Peter C. Ellmaker, the Naval Officer, who distinctly proves that Mr. Lewis was fully informed on the subject of the fictitious signatures, and that they formed a topic of conversation in the Custom House, between Mr. Lewis, Mr. Norris, George Read, and himself, long before the Collector was confirmed by the Senate. Mr. Ellmaker testifies as follows:

Q. Were you friendly to the confirmation of Mr. Lewis?
A. I was not opposed to it, sir, and I took no part in reference thereto.
Q. Were you friendly to the confirmation of Mr. Lewis?

A. I was friendly to it.

Q. When did you first hear, if you did hear, the subject of these fictitious signatures spoken of?

A. I am unable to state the time; it would be impossible to state when or how. *My impression is I heard it from Mr. Lewis prior to his confirmation.*

Q. Are you certain of the fact that you heard it from Mr. Lewis?

A. I am not *positively* certain, sir.

Q. Did you hear of it prior to the examination which took place before the Mayor of this city, on the subject?

A. My impression is that I did.

Q. How long before?

A. I am unable to say, sir.

Q. Was it a month before?

A. *It might have been a month, and might not have been a week.*

Q. Do you mean to say that you do not know whether it was a week or month before?

A. I do, sir.

Q. Where did you hear it?

A. My impression is that it was *in Mr. Lewis's office in the Custom House.*

Q. Who was present?

A. I don't know that any body was present at the time but Mr. Lewis and myself. *Mr. Norris might have been there, but I am not certain as to that fact.*

Q. From whom did Mr. Lewis say he heard it?

A. He did not give me the name of his informant.

Q. Why did he mention it to you?

A. I am unable to answer that question.

Q. Did he say why he mentioned it to you?

A. No sir, I think not.

Q. What did he say on the subject?

A. He said that *he intended investigating the matter, and that if fictitious or forged names had been signed to papers sent to Senators, by persons in the Weigher's office, as they had been charged with it, he would remove them.*

Q. Is that all he said?

A. *I don't remember, sir.*

Q. In what way did he communicate to you the fact, and in what language?

A. I don't understand the first part of that question: "in what way."

Q. Do you understand the latter part of it, in what language or words?

A. Yes, sir.

Q. Will you answer it?

A. I can't recollect the precise words which Mr. Lewis made use of on the occasion.

Q. State them as nearly as you can remember them.

A. I think I have stated already, as nearly as I can remember. I will repeat it with a great deal of pleasure.

Q. You have only stated what he said he intended to do, what did he say before that during that interview?

A. Mr. Lewis stated to me that he had learned—I don't use his precise words—that it had been charged in the Senate of the United States that forged or fictitious names had been signed in the Weigher's office, to papers which had been sent to senators recommending his confirmation, then followed what he stated he would do, as I have said, and it is unnecessary for me to repeat.

Q. Was there nothing said about the importance of contradicting this charge?

A. I do not remember.

Q. Was it not spoken of as, and considered to be a very serious matter?

A. Mr. Lewis, I have no doubt, considered it a serious matter. I don't remember that it was spoken of as a serious matter. Mr. Lewis no doubt considered it a serious matter or he would not have indicated the course which he said he intended to pursue by removing those implicated.

Q. Try and recollect, Mr. Ellmaker, if something was not said about the importance of contradicting the charge, either upon that or upon any other occasion.

A. I have stated already, Mr. Commissioner, what I remember, and I have no disposition to conceal anything that I know upon this subject. I have no recollection, sir, of any conversation of the kind more than I have detailed.

Q. How long were you and Mr. Lewis together upon that occasion?

A. We may have been together five minutes; five or ten minutes.

Q. Have you no recollection of any name or names being mentioned on that occasion in connection with fictitious signatures?

A. My impression is, that *Mr. Brady's name was mentioned, as the person by whom the charges could be proven.*

Q. Mr. Ellmaker, I wish you to state, if you can remember, all that was said upon that part of the subject, or as much of it as you can.

A. *I don't remember anything further, sir,* than what has already been stated.

* * * * * * *

Q. Was Geo. Read in the habit of visiting the Custom House frequently about that time?

A. I am unable to answer that question.

Q. Did you ever see him there?

A. Yes, sir.

Q. How often, in the course of a week?

A. I couldn't really tell how often in the course of a week. I believe he was and is generally there once a day.

Q. Were you not in the habit of seeing him there every day, prior to Mr. Lewis' confirmation?

A. I couldn't say; it is altogether likely he was there every day.

Q. Question renewed.

A. I have before stated that I cannot answer that question. My office is in a remote part of the building, and I am not in the habit of watching Mr. Read's movements.

Q. Why do you say, "it is altogether likely he was there every day"?

A. I say so because he has a desk in the building, at which his returns are made and his books are kept.

Q. Does he keep those books himself?

A. *I am not able to answer. I think* his books are kept by Mr. Fisler.

Q. Don't you know that they are kept by Mr. Fisler, Mr. Ellmaker?

A. I don't know it positively; it is my belief that they are.

Q. Don't you know that they are not kept by Mr. Read himself?

A. I have never seen Mr. Read making entries in them.

Q. Mr. Ellmaker, Yes or no will answer my question.

A. I should be very happy to answer Yes or no, if I could, but I am not in the habit of standing over Mr. Read, and watching his motions.

Q. Were you ever present when the fictitious signatures were spoken of by Mr. Lewis in the presence of Geo. Read?

A. My impression is, that Mr. Read was present; *I know he was present at the interview to which I referred in the Surveyor's office.*

Q. At any other time, sir, or place?

A. I don't remember, sir.

* * * * * * *

Q. Did you ever correspond with anybody on this subject?

A. *I don't think that I ever did, sir.* I would add, that during the pendency of Mr. Lewis' name in the senate, I studiously avoided taking any part in the controversy.

Q. Did Mr. Lewis himself ever write to you about the matter, or anything connected with it, during his absence in Washington?

A. *Yes, sir, I think Mr. Lewis has wrote to me perhaps two or three times.*

Q. Have you his letters, sir?

A. I have, sir, I think.

Q. Did you write to him?

A. I think I did, sir, once or twice. Mr. Lewis never wrote to me or I to him on the subject of the fictitious names; I did write to him on the subject of his confirmation, and he to me.

Q. Had that correspondence or any part of it, any relation to any charges which had been made in the Senate, against Mr. Lewis by Mr. McGrath or anybody else?

A. *I don't think it had.*

Q. Would you have any objection to produce those letters written you by Mr. Lewis?

A. I don't think I would feel authorized to produce private letters which I know can have no bearing upon this investigation.

* * * * * * *

Q. I think you have stated that the letters which you have referred to, relate to the question of the confirmation of Mr. Lewis; were they written before or after you heard of the fictitious signatures, and of the charge made against Mr. Lewis in the Senate in connection with them?

A. They were written *afterwards*, I think.

Mr. Gibbons requests the witness to produce the letters.

The witness declines producing them.

* * * * * * *

Q. Who was present when Mr. Lewis said he was going to remove Brady?

A. I have not yet said that Mr. Lewis said he was going to remove Brady. I said I was under the impression; I spoke of it as an impression.

Q. How did you derive that impression?

A. I think I have stated already that I was under the impression, that I heard it first from Mr. Lewis.

Q. I wish to know how you came by that impression?

A. *I will vary the word and say I believe I heard it from Mr. Lewis.*

Q. Now, sir, upon what do you found that *belief?*

A. *I decline answering the question.*

Q. Why?

A. I could not give an answer.

Q. Have you not any recollection of the fact?

A. I have none other than I have stated.

Q. Did you happen to know what he was to be removed for?

A. I will answer no. I do not *know* what he was removed for.

Q. Why do you emphasize the word "*know*" so strongly?

A. I heard it, from various sources, insinuated that Mr. Brady was to be removed, but I do not know that I heard the *cause* from Mr. Lewis.

Mr. Ellmaker's recollection of the conversations which occurred between Mr. Lewis, Mr. Norris, Read, and himself, in relation to the fictitious signatures, is very imperfect, but he brings home to Mr. Lewis and Mr. Norris, a full knowledge of the fact, *prior to the confirmation of the former by the Senate.* And, notwithstanding the asseveration of Mr. Brown to the contrary, he also swears that *Mr. Lewis mentioned the name of Mr. Brady to him "as the person by whom the charges could be proved."* But there is other evidence of the same facts. Mr. Brady testifies that before Mr. Lewis was confirmed, he called on Mr. Morton McMichael, *the friend of Mr. Lewis,* and made a full disclosure of the transactions to him. He then goes on to say:

"I was called by George Read into the Custom House a short time after I had communicated to Mr. McMichael, the facts of the fictitious signatures. I went into the Custom House with him. Mr. Read passed into the Collector's room, and I stood at Mr. Fisler's desk, nearly opposite the room. I saw Mr. Norris the Surveyor of the Port, in the room, and I thought I heard and knew Mr. McMichael's voice. I asked Mr. Fisler, who was writing at his desk by the gas light, what was going on in the Collector's room. He replied, "*there will be trouble,*" *the subject is about the fictitious names—it was in relation to what had happened in the Senate in reference to signing of fictitious names.* Mr. Lewis came out of the room—spoke to me, and passed on. He returned immediately, bowed to me again, and passed into the room. Mr. Fisler and I then walked home together."

Q. Did Mr. Lewis at any time make any inquiry of you in relation to the fictitious signatures?

A. Never. I asked for a hearing in my letter of the 14th of October; he never replied to it, and never gave me a hearing until the present time.

Mr. Lewis in his letter to the Secretary of the Treasury, dated Nov. 11th, 1850, written in reply to that which the Secretary had addressed to him on the 8th of the month *admits* that Mr. McMichael *did communicate to him in the month of August* the information which he had received from Mr. Brady, respecting the fictitious signatures. It was supposed that Mr. McMichael could bring to light the proceedings which were had on the subject at the meeting or caucus in the collector's room, at which he was present, and to which Mr. Brady refers. He was therefore subpœnaed as a witness on the part of the Government; and with what effect the oath of the officer will show.

Robert W. Jones, *sworn.*—"I am an officer connected with the office of Alderman Freeman. I served this subpœna on Mr. Morton McMichael, the Editor of the North American newspaper in this city. I saw him to-day—about half an hour since, in his office, about three, not four squares from this place. He said, 'say to the Commissioner and Alderman that I will not obey the summons.' He said he would like a copy of the subpœna for his own private use. Subpœna annexed as an Exhibit, and marked No. 17."

"Mr. Gibbons now makes application to the Commissioner for an attachment for Mr. McMichael, who has refused to obey the subpœna. The Commissioner decides that he has *no authority to issue an attachment.*"

The refusal of Mr. McMichael to disclose the secrets of his friend Mr. Lewis, leaves in the dark all that occurred in that caucus. Why Mr. Brady was invited into the Custom House on that occasion, and was permitted to retire without any examination or inquiry on the part of Mr. Lewis in relation to the fictitious names, which was the matter under consideration, is not explained. And why Mr. McMichael should refuse to reveal the proceedings of the caucus, *if they were of a character not prejudicial to Mr. Lewis in this investigation,* is a question which Mr. Lewis perhaps can answer. Every legal technicality which could be made available has been used by Mr. Brown in this investigation for the protection of his client; and in addition to that, we have now a suppression of evidence, which is utterly inconsistent with the averment that Mr.

Lewis is an innocent man. His friend, Mr. McMichael, refuses to be examined by the prosecution on a point which is vital to the defence, and his friend Mr. Ellmaker refuses to produce his correspondence. These are note-worthy facts, and they cannot be overlooked either in the discussion or in the final decision of this question. If the evidence which is suppressed, and which was entirely within the control of Mr. Lewis, could exonerate him, no man of common sense will believe that it would have been withheld. If it were but as a feather in his side of the balance, it would have been promptly produced, and magnified into any weight which his case required. There are other circumstances in this cause to which I shall presently advert, which authorize the opinion, that the object of the caucus was to concoct a scheme for the *effectual concealment of the fraud*, and that the correspondence with Mr. Ellmaker, while Mr. Lewis was at Washington, had relation to that scheme.

Mr. Lewis, in his letter to the Secretary of the Treasury of the 11th of November, (already cited), referring to the information which he had received from Mr. McMichael respecting the fictitious names says:

"During the long pendency of my nomination in the Senate, when every species of demerit was ascribed to me by my enemies and a portion of the disappointed applicants for office, I was called on by Morton McMichael, Esquire, probably about the latter end of August, who said that he had something that concerned me, of a very grave character, to communicate; he then informed me that Mr. Brady had called on him, and told him, that certain printed papers, to be addressed to Whig Senators vouching for my political orthodoxy, had been taken to the Weigher's office (which, it is proper to inform you is on the Wharf about a half a mile from the Custom House,) by Mr. Read, and that, by his directions and under his threats the whole Department had been engaged for months in signing them with the names of Citizens and forwarding them to Washington. Mr. McMichael said, *that if this were established he thought it would defeat my confirmation, and that it ought to be at once looked into.*"

* * * * * * * *

"Very soon after this I was informed, that Mr. Cooper expected to prove these forgeries through Francis E. Brady, and my connection with them, and that at Mr. Cooper's request, a week's delay in my case was granted by the Senate for that purpose, and to enable him to adduce other testimony to my disparagement."

The examination of witnesses on the subject, commenced before Mayor Jones on the 6th of September. It will be observed that *the caucus in the Custom House which was attended by Mr. Lewis, Mr. Norris, Mr. McMichael, and George Read, was held a few days only* prior to that date. At that investigation, some of the printed circulars, with the names attached, were produced, and an effort was made to obtain the attendance of Murray, Brady and Zane, as witnesses to prove that the names were signed in the Weigher's Office, and were spurious. But they did not appear, and consequently the fact was not established. The cause of their absence is now explained, as the following extracts from their testimony will show.

Mr. Brady testified as follows:—

Q. Did you ever happen to know of an investigation before the Mayor of this city, in relation to these fictitious signatures at any time while you held office, and if so from whom did you know it?

A. About the beginning of September last, I was told by George Read and Mr. Fisler, that an investigation was to take place before the Mayor. About the 2d or 3d of September, Mr. Fisler called on me, while I was on my duty on the wharf; *he stated that we must all swear, I mean the weighers, that we never knew or saw signed fictitious names to circulars in the Weigher's office.* Nobody was present but Mr. Fisler and myself. I told Mr. Fisler that I for one would not swear to any such thing; he stated that unless we did *it would be a defeat of Mr. Lewis' confirmation.* I told him no earthly power could induce me to perjure myself. We had considerable conversation on the subject, after which he went away. He called again the next day and asked me to join with all the weighers and do it; I still declined. He offered to deposite his year's salary to my credit if I would consent; I told him that the emoluments of the Custom House could not buy me to deliberately perjure myself. I told him I would resign my office, or I would leave the city until the depositions were closed. I asked him where Mr. Read was; he told me at the Custom House; I told him I would accompany him to see him. He stated that I would pity Read when I would see him. We went into the Custom House, Fisler and myself, and saw Mr. Read come out of Mr. Lewis' room, and he walked with me out of the Custom House front in Chestnut Street, and persisted in my complying with what Fisler requested me to do. I still declined, and told him I would go down and see Mr. McMichael, the Editor of the North American. It was then dark and we then separated.

* * * * * *

A. After I returned from Trenton, about the 9th or 10th of September, I saw Mr. Fisler and Mr. Read, I inquired what was done before the Mayor. Mr. Fisler told me that he was examined and *swore the matter through*, that George Read was not examined, nor Murray, nor Zane; that Zane ran off, and Murray *would not attend to the subpœna.* I asked him if he was examined upon the competency of the Weigh-master, George Read; he told me he was, and when they came out of the Mayor's office, Mr. Lewis said to Read, why don't you learn something; that he replied he had no time since Mr. Lewis' name was before the Senate.

Q. When did you go to Trenton, and how came you to go to Trenton?

A. On Thursday Morning, the 5th September last, I was weighing the cargo of a ship at Lombard Street wharf. Mr. Fisler called on me and asked me, "If you were brought up before the Mayor this morning and asked if you had signed any fictitious names to circulars in the Weigher's office, what answer will you make." My reply was, "I will tell the whole truth." He then asked me for my book, the book we weigh with, my cargo-book, and said I might go a rail shooting; George Read came up forward to me, I asked him if I might go; he said, "He didn't care a damn where I went." I turned to Mr. Fisler and asked him to give back my book, that I would stay; Mr. Read then said to me, "*Go*." I went to Trenton at half-past ten o'clock in the "New Philadelphia," that morning. I remained at Trenton and at Burlington until Saturday night.

"The depositions were closed on that day, as I heard from Read and Fisler, at the Weigher's office, on the Monday after my return from Trenton."

Mr. Murray's testimony on this point is as follows:

Q. Had you at any time any conversation with George Read or Charles H. Fisler about any examination before the Mayor on this subject?

A. The subject was mentioned in the office. I had received a summons whilst I was engaged on the wharf to appear before the Mayor in relation to the examination about fictitious names that took place last summer. I went to the Weigher's office—saw Mr. Read and Mr. Fisler and stated the circumstance of having received it. After some little conversation, I can't state what it was, I was told that ***I wasn't obliged to attend under that summons.*** I was told, I think by them both, Mr. Read and Mr. Fisler. I think that was the extent of the conversation at that time.

Q. During that conversation did either of them state to you what they wished you to swear to in case you should be examined?

A. I think not.

Q. Was there any conversation upon that subject?

A. There was. ***The substance of it was, that the transactions in the office should not be divulged.*** The conversation was a very short one, and I think that was the substance of it. I can't remember, exactly, what was said. They did not say what effect it would have upon the Senate. They wanted to know what I would testify to, in case I went up. I told them I did not think I would go up. I did not give them any satisfaction what I would say, further than that if I could help it I would not go before the Commissioner.

Mr. Zane, on the same point, says:

I was informed by Read and Fisler that a Committee would sit in this city, for the purpose of examining into the charge preferred in the Senate of the United States, that fictitious names had been signed in the Weigher's office to papers urging the confirmation of Mr. Lewis.

I was also told by Mr. Read that the matter must be sworn through. Mr. Read also informed me that Mr. Fisler was the only person attached to the Weigher's office examined on that occasion, *and he swore the matter through.* The latter part was stated after the examination before the Mayor; on the Sunday morning succeeding, at my own dwelling.

Q. At your first conversation, what was said in relation to your being examined as a witness?

A. *Mr. Read told me I must swear the matter through, if I did not, it would ruin me.*

Q. Was any thing said about your salary by Read.

A. There was. Mr. Read told me that if I would deny having signed any names that *he would place me on the same footing with others in the office—that my salary should be placed on the same footing as Mr. Murray and Mr. Fisler: each* of whom I knew received $1200 a year. From that I inferred that my salary would also be placed at $1200 a year.

Neither Brady, Murray, nor Zane appeared at the Mayor's office for examination, but Read and Fisler did appear with Mr. Lewis, and Fisler, to use his own words, "*swore the matter through.*" What is the plain deduction from the foregoing facts? Allow me to recapitulate them briefly. Some time before the examination took place before the Mayor, Mr. Lewis conversed with Mr. Ellmaker on the subject of the fictitious names, and "mentioned the name of Mr. Brady *as the person by whom the charges could be proved.*"

In the latter part of August, Mr. McMichael called on Mr. Lewis, told him what Brady had communicated to him, and said, (to use the language of Mr. Lewis himself,) "that if this were established, he thought *it would defeat my confirmation, and that it ought to be at once looked into.*"

Mr. Lewis soon after received information that the Senate had directed an inquiry into the facts, before the Mayor of Philadelphia.

Then followed the caucus in the Custom House attended by Lewis, Norris, Read and McMichael, "in relation (as Fisler stated) *to what had happened in the Senate* in reference to the signing of fictitious names."

Next in order is the application made by Fisler and Read, to Mr. Brady, *to attend* before the Mayor, and *swear the matter through.* In his conversation with Brady on the subject, Fisler uses the same idea which Mr. McMichael had suggested, that if the fact were established, *it would defeat the confirmation of Mr. Lewis.* This argument was not effective, and it was followed by a direct offer to bribe Mr. Brady to swear falsely. This also failed, and Brady was sent out of town, and did not return until the examination was over.

Murray and Zane are now informed that Mr. Lewis intends *to remove every person from office who had anything to do with the transaction,* and Read offers to raise Zane's salary to 1200 dollars a year, if he will deny that he had signed any fictitious names to the circulars. This attempt at bribery fails. Murray is told by Read and Fisler that the transactions in the Weigher's office *must not be divulged,* and he and Zane, both influenced by the *threat* of *a removal from office,* in case their participation in the affair should be made public by their examination, and advised that they were not bound to obey the subpœna, accordingly absent themselves.

Mr. Lewis well knowing that the other witnesses are out of the way, or will not appear, is very careful to bring forward Read and Fisler, and the latter confident that there is no one to contradict him, "*swears the matter through.*"

The manifest deduction from these facts, is, that Mr. Lewis regarded the concealment of the fraud as indispensable to secure his confirmation, that the plot for such concealment was concocted in that Custom House caucus, and that Read and Fisler were the agents designated and instructed by Mr. Lewis and Mr. Norris to carry it into effect at all hazards.

Mr. Lewis has always kept alive the threat, that he intended to *investigate the matter,* and to remove all who were concerned in it. He made this declaration to Mr. Ellmaker, prior to the examination of witnesses before the Mayor. If he intended to make an investigation, or desired one, why did he not require the attendance of Brady, Murray and Zane, upon that occasion? He admits in his letter to the Secretary of the Treasury already cited, that he was informed that an examination of the kind was intended. He had abundant time to notify all the officers connected with the Weigher's department to appear, and if he had been guiltless himself, he would have done so. But *he knew* that "*the matter could be proved by Brady,*" as he had told Mr. Ellmaker some time before, and he never *intended* hat an investigation should be made. He never did investigate it. He never exchanged a word with Mr. Brady on the subject. But he attached himself to Read and Fisler, the two unscrupulous men whom he could use for any purpose, and from the beginning to the end, he has leaned on them for safety. If the names were signed without his knowledge, why did he hesitate to send for Brady, Murray and Zane, when the fact was first disclosed to him, and learn whether they would confirm or deny the statements of Read and Fisler? Did his threat to remove all who were connected with the fraud, mean anything more than an intimation to those three officers, that there was no safety for them but *silence!* Surely not: and Mr. Brown admits it when he declares in his argument, that, Mr. Brady "*refused to confess to Mr. South because he knew from him and others, that Mr. Lewis had determined to probe the matter, and discharge all who were concerned in it!*"

It was not until after the publication of Mr. Brady's card, that Mr. Lewis ventured to speak either to Murray or Zane on the subject. I read now from his letter of the 11th of November, to the Secretary of the Treasury.

"On my return from Washington, after my confirmation, and when I thought the proper time had arrived, I had an interview with the other two Deputy Weighers, John E. Murray and Joel Zane, and inquired of them whether any such signing of names as I had been told Mr. Brady had reported, had taken place in the Weigher's Office, and if so, under what circumstances and to what extent.

"I beg you to observe that this was the *first time* I had spoken with either of the deputies on this subject. Mr. Murray told me that all he knew of any such signing, and all the agency he had in it, was, that he had written two, or at most three names to one of the papers of persons who he was told wished them placed there.

"Mr. Zane informed me that all he knew upon the subject, was, that he had in like manner written the names of four, possibly six persons who had authorized him to sign for them, but that he had obtained to the papers the signatures of at least five hundred persons whom he had asked to sign: both stated that they had no knowledge of any of the other persons employed in the office having written names to papers of any kind, or having been required by the Chief Weigher to do so."

Now it might be supposed from the first paragraph above cited from Mr. Lewis' letter, that he began "to probe this matter," immediately after his confirmation; and he evidently intended that the Secretary of the Treasury should so understand it. But by turning to the testimony of Mr. Murray and Mr. Zane, it will be found that he had no communication whatever with them on the subject, *until after he had determined to remove Mr. Brady*, and had communicated his intention to Mr. Ellmaker, who mentioned it to Mr. Samuel Allen, by whom Mr. Brady was informed of the fact. Mr. Brady immediately addressed to Mr. Lewis the letter which appears in his card, (dated Oct. 14, 1850,) and in which he desired a hearing on the subject. *It was on the day after Mr. Lewis received the letter*, that he and Mr. Norris called on Mr. Zane and Mr. Murray, *not to investigate the matter*, but to ascertain whether *they* had signed any fictitious names. This inquiry was made while the threat hung over them, that Mr. Lewis would remove every body who was connected with the matter. Murray and Zane were therefore asked to convict themselves without promise of pardon, and as might be expected they gave evasive but *pregnant* answers to Mr. Lewis' question.

Both of them testify that he carried his inquiry no further, and that *Read and Fisler* were kept out of view entirely. Neither of them told Mr. Lewis on that, or on any other occasion, that "they had no knowledge of any of the other persons employed in the office having written names to papers of any kind, or having been required by the Chief Weigher to do so." Mr. Lewis asserts this in his letter to the Secretary, and both of the witnesses flatly contradict him. He did not speak *to Mr. Brady on the subject*, although he was there at the time, was seen by him, and was within the sound of his voice.

After Mr. Brady's removal, and the publication of his card, and before Mr. Lewis received the letter of the Secretary of the Treasury, dated the 8th of November, he had another conversation with both Mr. Murray and Mr. Zane, in his own room at the Custom House. On that occasion he examined them separately, and each *confirmed* the material facts alleged in the publication of Mr. Brady. Mr. Murray stated to him *all the facts which he has testified to in this investigation.* He told him that he had seen Read hand out the circulars for the purpose of having the names appended, and that the names which he signed, were signed by Read's request. He further stated that it was his belief that a large number of fictitious names had been signed to the circulars. Mr. Lewis, in possession of all this information from Mr. Murray, wrote *with his own hand,* the form of an affidavit, which Mr. Murray copied in his presence, and swore to, by his request. That affidavit is as follows:

"I, John E. Murray, Deputy Weigher, having read the card of Francis E. Brady, which appeared in the Sunday Dispatch of the 3d inst., do hereby declare, that Geo. Read, the Chief Weigher, never directed me to sign as many names as I could to printed circulars addressed to Senators, recommending Mr. Lewis, the Collector, for confirmation; nor did any conversation of Mr. Read with any persons in the Weigher's office, such as Mr. Brady describes in his card, occur in my presence. My impression is that some names were written to those papers in the Weigher's office, though I cannot designate any person as having written them, nor did I see any such names put upon the paper. I did, however, myself write down on one of the papers the names of two or three persons at furthest, who were desirous, as I was informed, of having them placed there.

Sworn to Nov. 8, 1850. "JNO. E. MURRAY."

This is one of the affidavits sent to the Department by Mr. Lewis, in his letter of the 11th November. The affidavit is true, *as far as it goes*, but it will be observed that it is so worded as to *conceal* the very facts respecting which an explanation had been demanded by the President. Why did Mr. Lewis desire to screen his friend Geo. Read, by introducing the words, "George Read, the chief Weigher, *never* directed me to sign *as many names as I could*," &c., and omit to state that he did direct or request the deponent to sign those to which he refers? Why did he omit to state that Read handed out the circulars in the Weigher's office, for the purpose of having the fictitious names attached to them?

Mr. Lewis desired to go even a step further. His original draft of Murray's affidavit, which will be found annexed to the depositions, as Exhibit No. 15, contains the following sentence:

"I declare further that I did not see *Mr. Fisler*, one of the other Deputies, or any other person sign names to those papers in the Weigher's office, or elsewhere."

Mr. Murray, however, *declined swearing to that paragraph, and it was erased.* This incident is worthy of note, because it tends to show the extreme anxiety of Mr. Lewis to *protect* both Fisler and Read.

On the same day that Murray made his affidavit, being the 8th of the month, Mr. Lewis had his second conversation with Mr. Zane, who testifies as follows:

"I then disclosed to him the whole matter of signing fictitious names; told him that there had been names signed in the Weigher's office, that I had signed some, Mr. Brady had signed, and Fisler: that the city directory was handed to Mr. Brady, as stated in his card; that Mr. Read had threatened that any person who refused to sign those names, was unfriendly to Mr. Lewis, and would be removed from office."

An affidavit had been prepared for Mr. Zane, contradicting the statements in Brady's card, the draft of which is annexed to the depositions, marked Exhibit No. 16. It is in the following words:

"I, Joel Zane, Deputy Weigher, having read Mr. Brady's card, in which he asserts that persons employed in the Weigher's office had signed, or had been required by Mr. Read to sign fictitious or other names to certain printed circulars to senators, recommending Mr. Lewis our collector, for confirmation, declare that I have no knowledge of any such requisition having been made by Mr. Read [nor of any persons having affixed to such circulars fictitious or forged signatures.

"I appended myself to one of them the names of four, possibly of six, persons friendly to Mr. Lewis, having been authorized to do so, but am very certain the number put down by me did not exceed six.

"The circulars were very numerously and generally signed, few members of the Whig party who were asked to sign them having refused to do so.

["I also declare that I was on my way to the Mayor's office in company with Mr. Murray, to testify in the matter referred to when we learned that the Commissioner had adjourned.]

"PHILADELPHIA, November 8th, 1850.

"I also declare that Mr. Brady told me, that if he was sacrificed in this business, he was promised a better place at Washington, though Mr. Cooper's influence."

The last paragraph is in the handwriting of Mr. Lewis. He exhibited this paper to Mr. Zane during the interview, but he declined swearing to it, on the ground that it was not true. After he had made the foregoing disclosure to Mr. Lewis, he was permitted to depart, and was not invited to make any written statement on the subject.

On the following day *Mr. Fisler*, by direction of Mr. Lewis, *made an affidavit contradicting the entire statement of Mr. Brady*, which he placed in Mr. Lewis' hands. Two days afterwards, being the 11th of November, an affidavit was prepared for George Read of a like character, which he swore to, and gave to Mr. Lewis. Whether Read knew the contents of his affidavit has not been proved, but it contains (*inter alia*) the following remarkable passage.

"But if I were as illiterate as he (Mr. Brady) would make me appear, for he asserts twice in his card, that I can can neither read nor write, I should hardly have been considered fit to serve, as I did without discredit between two or three years, as Treasurer of the County of Philadelphia, or to have been twice elected a commissioner of the District of Kensington, in which capacity I served six years," &c.

Whether Mr. Lewis prepared this affidavit or not, he knew the contents of it before it was sworn to; and, *he knew as well as any living man, that George Read could neither read nor write.* Yet he did not hesitate to attempt to deceive the President by the use of language, which would lead to an opposite inference, and permit that language to be verified by an oath! The affidavits which Mr. Lewis thus obtained from Murray, Fisler, and Read, were forwarded by him to the Secretary of the Treasury in his letter dated Nov. 11. 1850—which concludes as follows: "Deeming it probable that you might expect a refutation of Brady's statements, I called upon the persons implicated, to clear their skirts of his charges in a formal manner. My call has been answered by the weigher and two of his deputies, in the form of affidavits, transmitted herewith. *Mr. Zane has not yet answered the call. His statement shall be forwarded as soon as received.*"

It will be observed that Mr. Zane had *answered the call, three days prior to the date of Mr. Lewis's letter.* But the answer did not suit the purpose of Mr. Lewis, and he did not apply to Mr. Zane for his *affidavit* until *after* he had despatched the other affidavits to the Secretary of the Treasury. The object of this will presently appear.

After he had mailed his letter of the 11th inst., to the Secretary of the Treasury, he addressed the following note to Mr. Zane.

CUSTOM HOUSE, *Philadelphia*,
Collector's Office, Nov. 11th, 1850.

SIR:

I find it my duty to call upon you for a statement under oath of your knowledge, if any, concerning the charges against the United States Weighers and Deputies of this District contained in a "Card," signed Francis E. Brady, which appeared in the "Sunday Dispatch," of the 3d inst.

Yours, respectfully,
WM. D. LEWIS, Collector.

JOEL ZANE, Esquire, United States
Deputy Weigher, No. 23, Arch street.

Mr. Zane received this note on the evening of the 11th of November, and called on Mr. Lewis the next day, when he read to him the letter which he had received from the Secretary of the Treasury, dated Nov. 8th, 1850. He requested him to make an affidavit, and gave him leave of absence for the day to enable him to do it. On the following day, (the 13th,) he again called on Mr. Lewis, handed him a copy of the statement which he had prepared, which Mr. Lewis read, and suggested some alterations. The statement, with the alterations proposed will be found annexed to the testimony marked "Exhibit No. 4." The witness further says,

"In my conversation with Mr. Lewis, he asked me whether I thought *Mr. Read was really in earnest when he handed the Directory to Mr. Brady.* I told him that I could hardly say whether he was or not, as I was engaged at the time. I wrote the words '*in a jocose manner*,' (interlined on the Exhibit No. 4) told Mr. Lewis that I would take the paper home with me, would reflect upon the matter, would carefully examine my mind on that point, and if I could conscientiously insert those words I would do so. On the next day Mr. Lewis remarked that I had not inserted those words in the affidavit which I had actually made. I replied to him that in my affidavit I had confined myself exclusively to facts which came under my own knowledge." The witness also testifies, that after he had made his affidavit and handed it to Mr. Lewis, *Mr. Lewis wrote on another paper the postscript* to the affidavit, which Mr. Zane, by his request, copied and swore to.—The P. S. is in the following words:

"P. S. I feel it due to you to state that when you called upon me in reference to this matter, prior to Mr. Brady's removal, the facts set forth in this affidavit were not made known to you. My reason for withholding them was an unwillingness to implicate persons in the office with me."

Very respectfully,

JOEL ZANE.

Sworn and subscribed before C. D. Freeman, Nov. 14, 1850,

The postscript is *literally true*, but it is very far from being the whole truth. It is true that Mr. Zane did not communicate to Mr. Lewis *"the facts set forth in the affidavit,"* prior to Mr. Brady's removal, but he did communicate to him *some of those facts*, and would probably have communicated *all of them*, if Mr. Lewis had desired or requested it. It has already been shown, that *seven days before the postscript was written by Mr. Lewis*, and three days before Mr. Lewis' letter to the Secretary of the 11th, Mr. Zane had made to him a *full disclosure*.

On the 14th November, 1850, Mr. Lewis forwarded the affidavit of Mr. Zane to the Secretary of the Treasury, enclosed in the following letter:

Custom House, *Philadelphia*,
Collector's Office, Nov. 14, 1850.

Sir:

Referring you to my letter of the 11th inst., I transmit herewith a copy of a letter addressed by me to Joel Zane, United States Deputy Weigher, on that day, marked A., and his statement under Oath, in reply, received this morning, marked B., in relation to the charges contained in the Brady "Card." I trust the P. S. to Mr. Zane's statement, will not escape your attention.

I also send herewith a communication received this day from George Read, marked C., covering the Documents marked 1, 2, and 3, and, also a letter from Charles H. Fisler, marked D., enclosing the paper marked A., and remain very respectfully,

WM. D. LEWIS, Collector.

Hon. Thomas Corwin, Secretary of the Treasury, *Washington, D. C.*

The two concluding paragraphs of this letter are worthy of note. Mr. Lewis trusts "that the P. S. to Mr. Zane's statement," *which was prepared by his own hand*, "will not escape the attention" of the Secretary! Can any thing be more apparent than this persevering attempt to conceal from the department, the knowledge which he had of the facts of this case, even after the President had called for an explanation? Would not an innocent man in answer to such a demand, have scorned the artifices which have been exposed here, in making his defence! Why was not the affidavit of Mr. Zane obtained by Mr. Lewis at their first interview in the Custom House, and sent to the department with the others, on the 11th of the month? The last paragraph in his letter of the 14th, exposes the base motive in withholding it. It would have been sending the antidote with the poison which he was administering to the President. He therefore held it back until his friends Read and Fisler could get up the "testimonials," to which I have heretofore particularly referred, signed by individuals whom they were *afraid to call* as witnesses in this proceeding, well knowing that not one of them would be willing to sustain under oath the statements to which they had carelessly and inadvertently placed their names. These were designed not only to *strengthen* the faith of the President in the affidavits of Read and Fisler, and to deceive him on the question of the competency of the former, but were sent in company with the affidavit of Zane to *neutralize* its effect, for he was introduced without friends and without compurgators!

I deem it unnecessary to extend this reply to the argument of Mr. Brown. The facts which are before the Department appear to me to sustain fully, and beyond all reasonable doubt, the second specification. It has been proved that fictitious names were signed: some of the circulars so signed are attached to the testimony, and it has been proved that those identical papers were sent to members of the Senate, and were seen and handled by Mr. Lewis during the examination before the Mayor, and that prior to that time he knew the whole story. It has been proved by the repeated declarations of Read, that he carried all the papers which had been fraudulently signed to the Custom House, as fast as he obtained them, and Mr. Lewis, in his conversation with Zane, stated that *all the circulars had been forwarded to Washington by Mr. Norris.* It has been proved that from the time of his first conversation with Ellmaker, to the publication of Brady's card, Mr. Lewis constantly declared that he meant to investigate the matter, and remove from office all who were connected with it, but that, instead of investigating it, his whole effort was to *conceal it,* and that his threat was only intended to *prevent* a confirmation of the charge, by intimidating Mr. Zane and Mr. Murray into silence. His close and intimate association with Read and Fisler, and his effort to sustain them on all occasions, has been clearly and satisfactorily proved. His repeated attempts to deceive the President are manifest in every step which he has taken in this proceeding. I shall not dwell upon it longer—nor recapitulate the points which I have made in this hasty and imperfect answer to the argument which has been filed by the opposite counsel. To use the language of the Secretary of the Treasury, in a somewhat modified form, " the disclosures made by the testimony are of a character to shock the moral sense of the public, and no consideration should protect the *instigators* of such enormities from such punishment as public or social law can inflict."

Read and Fisler are retained in office. Mr. William D. Lewis has taken them under his own wings. They are kept warm, and snug, and comfortable by the congenial exhalations from his own breast. If they had sprung from his own loins they could not be greater objects of his solicitude and care. But virtue sickens and dies in the miasma which surrounds them, and the brilliant talent of their counsel, immersed in it for a moment, looses its lustre, its refinement, and its power!

CHARLES GIBBONS,
For Complainants.

PREFACE.

The following answer to the Narrative of William D. Lewis, was prepared by Senator Cooper in February last, and delivered to the President about the adjournment of Congress. It will be found to contain a full and complete refutation of the statements of said Narrative, exhibiting the motives, and exposing the misrepresentations of Mr. Lewis, in a manner that must satisfy every unbiassed reader, of the falsity of the charges brought against Mr. Cooper by Mr. Lewis. "Oh! that mine enemy would write a book," was the exclamation of a wise man of old; and never had any one occasion for more thankfulness that his enemy had done so, than has Mr. Cooper in this instance. It has furnished him, not only with an opportunity to vindicate himself from calumnies which were whispered in secret, but to turn upon his enemy and smite him to the earth with his own weapons. This he has done, and in a manner which renders it difficult to say, which is the most complete, his vindication of himself, or the prostration of his vindictive assailant. Hypocrisy, falsehood, malevolence and meanness, have all been fixed upon the latter, and branded upon his character, leaving dishonoring scars never to be effaced whilst the memory of his transactions survive.

In this statement, Mr. Cooper exhibits Mr. Lewis as a sycophant, courting his favor by the pretence of rejoicing at his election to the United States Senate; guilty of deliberate and wilful misrepresentation, in ascribing the appointment of George Read to his recommendation and influence; and of meanness, in endeavoring to shift the responsibility of that act upon others. His attempt, through the instrumentality of his friend Levin, to impose upon the Senate by false assertions and discreditable contrivances, as well as his transactions with Harris & Co., and the Messrs. Whitney, as detailed by Mr. Cooper, are not only exposed, but seem to defy explanation. He has, in short, struggled in vain to withdraw the attention of the public from his guilt of the charges preferred against him by a number of highly respectable citizens of Philadelphia; and his impotent assault upon the character of Mr. Cooper, whose only indiscretion seems to have been that, even for a brief period, he suffered Lewis, Levin, South, and Read to be on terms of intimacy with him, has but served to expose the more his real character to the public. His own Narrative, by its pitiful subterfuges, unwarrantable deductions, and palpable attempt to mislead and deceive, was sufficient to place him in the pillory of public opinion, an object of derision to the passers by; but the statement made by Mr. Cooper in reply, has nailed his ears to the post, and placed his feet in the stocks. This is his reward for writing a book.

REPLY OF MR. COOPER

To the Narrative of William D. Lewis, appended to the Record of the proceedings of the Commissioner appointed to investigate the charges preferred against him by certain Citizens of the City and County of Philadelphia.

The attack made upon me by Mr. William D. Lewis, in a paper annexed to the proceedings before the Commissioner, and which he styles his "narrative," would have been considered unworthy of notice, and disregarded, were it not that it is to become a permanent record, which will bear testimony that may affect others, after both he and I shall have gone to account at a higher and more unerring tribunal, than even that of public opinion. To those who are acquainted with the object of this "narrative," the motives of its author, and the circumstances under which it was presented, no answer to its manifold falsehoods would be necessary. It was uncalled for, and without purpose, as far as the late investigation was concerned. There is no attempt to explain the testimony, to impeach its credibility, or to defend himself against the charges which were preferred. If any such thing be intended by Mr. Lewis, as to assail the character and credibility of the witnesses, or to defend himself, it is to be done *secretly*, in the absence of his accusers, and where no opportunity to answer him will be afforded. A discussion, of the facts disclosed by the investigation, he knows well, would end in his deeper degradation and more overwhelming disgrace. Hence his indisposition to refer to the subject; hence his attempt to withdraw the attention of those who are to judge him, from the true issue, by a bootless attack upon me.

His "narrative" has no relation to the matter at issue, contains no defence against the charges preferred, nor any explanation of the evidence produced. In it, he does not pretend to exculpate himself. Too sagacious to attempt that which is impossible, he shrewdly endeavors to withdraw attention from his own turpitude, at the same time that he gratifies his malice by calumniating me. In thus assailing me, he is carrying out a purpose long ago expressed. More than a year since, he avowed his intention to destroy me, if possible, in language the most profane and offensive; and the industrious vindictiveness with which he has pursued his purpose, in this respect, proves, that although truth is by no means one of his distinguishing characteristics, he nevertheless sometimes keeps his word. The language used, as near as I can recollect it, was as follows: "Cooper has determined to oppose me; well, God damn him, let him do so. I will destroy him; I am too old for him, and that he will find out. I crossed the Atlantic to kill Leavitt Harris, when he was appointed Minister to Russia, and by God I would do the same to break down Cooper, if it were necessary." See letter of Thomas E. Crowell, Esq., annexed, and marked A.*

This, taken in connection with his conduct generally, shows the motive which induced Mr. Lewis to disregard the necessities of his own case, by assailing me in a statement false in every material particular, from beginning to end. Having thus shown the motives by which he is actuated—that his malice is so bitter and vindictive, that to gratify it, wary and selfish as he is known to be, he has overlooked his own interests, and left without reply, testimony implicating him in a gross fraud, and steeping him to the lips in dishonor, I might content myself without further reply to the outpouring of his malevolence. But I, too, have a "narrative," which I not only wish to put on record, but to exhibit to the public; and like Mr. Lewis, in this particular, though I trust in no other, I shall begin with a history of the contest for the Collectorship.

Before the inauguration of General Taylor, in March, 1849, a number of applicants presented themselves for the Collectorship, amongst whom were Governor Ramsey, General Peter Sken Smith, Charles Gilpin, John S. Riddle, Edward C. Dale, William D. Lewis, and perhaps some others. With the exception of General Smith, who was a Native American, and Mr. Lewis, whose political opinions were not very well defined, and whose relation to the two great parties of the country, resembled that of the "cow boys" to the Whigs and Tories of the Revolution, who sold beef to both, the gentlemen named were all active Whigs of high standing, and deservedly esteemed. Of Mr. Lewis, at that time, I knew little, having met him but once, some two or three years previously, on the street, and never afterwards had any communication with him, except through the medium of a very laconic telegraphic despatch, addressed by him to me, the night after my election to the United

* This letter has since been procured, and is annexed to the copy of this paper in the hands of the President.

States Senate. It contained but two words, "*Thank God!*" by way of congratulation for my success; and I was very much surprised at the receipt of it, having understood that Mr. Lewis had manifested great anxiety in behalf of one of my prominent competitors. Some time afterwards, when I mentioned the circumstance to the gentleman referred to, and inquired if he knew what part Mr. Lewis had taken, he replied, jocosely, "Had I been elected, you would have saved two cents, and I would have got the despatch,"—meaning, that the "Thank God" of Mr. Lewis was for the winner, whoever he might be.

It is true, that previously to this time, I was aware of the failure of the Girard Bank, and had heard, that while he had acquired a princely fortune, many of the stockholders had become bankrupt. I was aware, also, that a Committee of the stockholders had pronounced his conduct free from blame; but I was equally aware that the community still continued to regard him as the author of the misfortunes of the institution, and that the distress of plundered widows, and the cry of beggared orphans had neither been assuaged nor quieted by the report. And as it was universally known, in Philadelphia, that Mr. Lewis had unlimited control in the management of the Bank, that nearly all of its capital had been sunk, and a large number of the stockholders ruined, the testimony borne by the report to his faithful, judicious, and upright conduct, in the administration of its affairs, went but a little way to relieve him from the load of suspicion which has weighed upon him from that day to this. It was known how easy it is, for an adroit man, powerful by his wealth, unscrupulous as to means, and necessarily informed in advance of any impending catastrophe, to guard against its consequences, and provide for his own exculpation. This, it may be presumed, Mr. Lewis had taken the precaution to do. His friends, those immediately connected and acting with him, would be on the ground, ready, active, and in possession of the means to carry out his purposes; while those who were not in his confidence, the "uninitiated," and those living at a distance, would be virtually excluded from any participation in the steps taken, by the more interested parties, to justify him. And it has not failed to be remarked, that notwithstanding the assertion of the report, that the conduct of the Cashier, in the management of the Bank, was wise, faithful, discreet, and upright, a rich corporation, with a real capital of millions, almost solely under his control, became bankrupt and its stockholders ruined, whilst *he became rich.* A committee, constituted as committees of this kind usually are, might exonerate Mr. Lewis, but not change the opinion of the community in regard to him; and there is one striking fact, notwithstanding the report, viz.: that going into the institution poor, he left it rich; whilst hundreds who entered it rich, came out of it beggared!

In the contest for Collector, I was the undisguised, open, earnest supporter of Governor Ramsey, and every body, connected in any way with the subject, knew me to be so. I pressed his appointment on the President with zeal; and continued to do so, until I learned from him that he had determined to appoint a city merchant. To support Mr. Lewis, I could never bring my mind; though I was urged to do so in the most earnest manner, especially by Mr. Henry White, to whom I was under obligations for acts of political friendship, and whom I would have been happy to serve. Mr. Lewis, however, asserts in his "narrative," that "I addressed to a member of Congress, a letter to be used with the President in promoting his appointment, and that on the same day, I had furnished the same member with a letter equally strong, in favor of another applicant for the same place," &c. This assertion is utterly false, and in addition to this, it is absurd. The member of Congress referred to, is Lewis C. Levin, the confidential and bosom friend of Mr. Lewis, and who acted as the agent of the latter during the whole of the time his nomination was pending before the Senate. It has long since become a standing maxim of the world's wisdom, that a man shall be judged by the company he keeps. If the maxim be a just one, Mr. Lewis, in view of his relations with Mr. Levin, and others like him, would do well to show, that he ought to be excepted from its application.

But this is not the first time that Mr. Lewis has endeavored to make use of these letters; though I suspect it will be the last. One of them was produced in the Senate, whilst his confirmation was pending there, attended by circumstances which would have put to shame, any one who had any of that feeling left. The history of these letters is briefly this.

On the 9th of April, 1849, according to the best of my recollection as to the date, being in Philadelphia, I received a letter from Levin, requesting me to make inquiry and furnish him, for his own private information and guidance, answers to certain interrogatories, which were substantially as follows:—"Who do Mr. Henry White, A. J. Lewis, Frederick Lennig, Francis N. Buck, and probably some others, support for the office of Collector? What is their standing as gentlemen and Whigs? What weight should be given to their recommendations? Is Mr. Lewis popular or otherwise; and what effect would it have in my own district, were I to urge his appointment?" There was something in the character of this letter which struck me as strange at the time of its receipt. My acquaintance with its author was of very recent date, and his knowledge of Philadelphia much more extensive than mine. I was therefore surprised at the inquiries addressed to me; and the more so, that when I left Washington a few days before, he was an advocate of the appointment of Mr. Dale. But being disposed to accommodate him, after informing myself on the subject, for I knew nothing of the state of public feeling in the city, of my own knowledge, I answered, as nearly as I can recollect, as follows:—"Mr. White, and the other gentlemen named by you, are supporters of William D. Lewis; they are all gentlemen of high standing, whose recommendations deserve to be treated with respectful consideration. The sentiment in favor of Mr. Lewis is strong; and you need have no apprehensions in advocating the appointment of a man who is supported by Henry White and others like him."

It is necessary to observe, that I knew nothing of the state of public sentiment in Philadelphia, in relation to the Collectorship, of my own knowledge, not having been there for many months, except, perhaps, stopping over night on my way to Pottsville. And of this, I am not quite sure, not recollecting precisely the date of the letter. The information which I received, was from an intelligent gentleman, who professed to be neutral on the subject of the Collectorship, but who has since taken an active part in favor of Mr. Lewis. The information I received from him, I transmitted to Mr. Levin, who knew well that it was not designed as a recommendation of Mr. Lewis, on my part; nor did he ever use it, or even speak of it as such, publicly, until after the death of General Taylor. Shortly after the commencement of the last session of Congress, and after he had become satisfied that my determination to oppose the confirmation of Mr. Lewis could not be changed, I was informed that he had been whispering it about, that I had recommended him, and that he had in his possession a letter to that effect, which he had shown to General Taylor. In consequence of this information, I called on Levin, and asked him, whether he had ever made such an assertion, or shown any letter of mine to the President, or stated to him that he was in possession of a letter of mine, recommending Mr. Lewis? He denied it all, emphatically and unequivocally; and to disprove the portion of the charge, which referred to his exhibition of it to the President, and of his statement to him that he had such a letter, he insisted on my accompanying him to see Gen. Taylor. We accordingly went, and the President stated, in answer to an interrogatory of Mr. Levin, to that effect, *that he had never seen or heard of such a letter!* After the death of the President, there being no longer a witness, whose testimony would give the lie to his assertions, he commenced exhibiting the letter, declaring that it was designed as a recommendation of Mr. Lewis. I need not characterize his conduct. His own acts paint it in colors darker than language could do.

But, if I desired the appointment of Mr. Lewis, why take this awkward way to accomplish it? Why not address the President at once (as I was doing at the time in favor of another), or some of the members of his Cabinet, with all of whom I was acquainted? Why select Levin as the medium of communicating my wishes; and why above all put myself in his power by acting the somewhat worse than stupid part ascribed to me?

It is said, however, that my design was to secure the favor of Mr. Lewis; but when Mr. Lewis made this assertion he knew it to be untrue. When he called on me in Philadelphia, after his appointment, and the withdrawal of my recommendation of George Read, as I shall show hereafter, I told him in the most explicit terms that I had not favored his appointment. If, as alleged, I had written two letters, one for, and another against him, both of which were in the hands of his confidential friend and agent, Levin, could I with any reason expect he would not be informed of it? The story bears upon its face the impress both of absurdity and falsehood.

The above mentioned letter was produced in the Senate whilst Mr. Lewis' nomination was under consideration, with an explanation, furnished by Mr. Levin, somewhat similar to that contained in the "narrative;" but it was accompanied by sundry little accessories which Mr. Lewis has omitted to mention—not through ignorance, for of the doings in the Senate he professes to be well informed. It was stated there, on the authority of Mr. Levin, that I had written two letters, the one in question recommending Mr. Lewis, the other recommending Mr. Dale; that they were *both* written in Philadelphia on the same day, delivered to him there, and not sent by mail, as I had asserted in my place in the Senate, the day previously. To help out this falsehood and make it effectual for its purpose, corroborating circumstances were deemed necessary; and these Mr. Levin prepared. Instead of the original envelope in which the letter had been sent, another was procured and shown without post mark, and without address as to place. But unfortunately for the contriver of the fraud, the envelope was a Congressional one, and directed by Levin *to himself in his own hand-writing!* This can be proved by a number of Senators who were present when the fraud was detected.

It is true, as the "narrative" asserts, that I did write a letter to Mr. Levin, in relation to the supporters of Mr. Dale, their standing, &c., in reply to one which I received from him of like purport with the one in relation to Mr. Lewis. But that it was on the same day, as asserted by Mr. Lewis and his coadjutor Mr. Levin, is false, utterly and wholly false; and in proof of the falsehood I challenge its production now, as I did in the Senate, when its existence was mentioned there, on the authority of the latter. But the non-production of the letter is not the only proof of Mr. Levin's part of the falsehood. He asserted that both letters were written in Philadelphia on the same day, and delivered to him there. But in the examination which took place before the Mayor of Philadelphia, Thomas E. Crowell, Esq., swears that Mr. Levin told him the letter in relation to Mr. Lewis was received by him in Washington, in reply to one addressed by him from thence. Thus Mr. Levin is convicted of falsehood out of his own mouth, to say nothing of the forgery of the envelope and the direction upon it, or of the intrinsic marks of falsehood which the whole story bears upon its face. See Crowell's deposition annexed, and marked L.*

There are other facts to which I have briefly adverted, which prove that I either courted the exposure of the double-dealing, charged upon me by Mr. Lewis and Mr. Levin, or that the charge itself is false. While it is alleged that I had written a letter recommending Mr. Lewis, and which I could hardly presume would not be shown to the President, if it had been designed as a recommendation, I was engaged in pressing upon him personally the appointment of another. After learning from him that he had determined to appoint a city merchant, that Governor Ramsey was out of the question, and that he would never under any circumstances appoint Mr. Lewis, I presented to him the name of Mr. Joseph B. Myers, and urged his appointment earnestly and zealously. At the time I did this, Josiah Randall, Esq., was present, and can bear testimony to the fact. Mr. Myers, who had not been consulted, on learning from me that his name had been presented, declined to per-

* This deposition is annexed to the copy of this paper in the hands of the President.

mit it to be further used. After his declination, I became the supporter of Mr. Dale, and spoke to the President in his behalf. Under such circumstances, is it probable, that I could have written a letter in favor of Mr. Lewis, designed either to reccommend him to the President, or secure his goodwill in the event of his appointment? Could I suppose the President would remain ignorant of such a letter, informed as I was of the something more than mere friendly zeal which animated Levin in favor of Mr. Lewis? And assured of this, would I have exposed myself to his contempt by writing in favor of Mr. Lewis, whilst I was urging another upon him personally?

Again. It is alleged, that I had written two letters, one in favor of Lewis and the other in favor of Dale,* and that they were in possession of Levin—indeed, that they had been both written and delivered to him on the same day. And I did this to win the favor of Mr. Lewis—win it by writing a letter urging his most formidable competitor, and placing it in the hands of his most devoted friend, who, according to his own statement, had a bargain with him before he agreed to support him, that he should have the naming of one-third of his appointees!† Is this credible? Might I not just as well have sought Mr. Lewis' favor by writing a letter in behalf of Mr. Dale, and placing it in Mr. Lewis' hands as in those of Mr. Levin, his agent and confidential friend?

But further;—having previously learned the determination of the President not to nominate Mr. Lewis, I was not aware that he had reconsidered it up to the moment when Mr. Lewis was appointed. His declarations not to appoint him were so decided and unequivocal, and repeated with asseverations of his determination not to do it, so solemn, that it never entered my mind that his could change. As I have stated before, Josiah Randall, Esq., was witness to these declarations of the President—declarations so broad, and so strong as to admit of no contingency favorable to Mr. Lewis. [See Letter marked X.] He stated distinctly, and repeated it more than once, that he must not only be innocent, but free from the suspicion of guilt involved in the charges preferred against him—that he would appoint no one to an office of such responsibility as that for which Mr. Lewis was an applicant, who had been connected in any manner with insolvent Banks; and that howsoever honest he might be, the suspi-

* I do not recollect which letter was first written, but believe it was the one relative to Mr. Lewis.

† See Levin's speech in Appendix.

cion that he had been, or might be otherwise, would prove injurious to the administration and preclude his appointment on the rules which he had prescribed for his government.

Before taking leave of this part of the subject, it is proper to remark, that at the urgent instance of Mr. Henry White, for whom I entertained great respect, I had forborne to oppose the appointment of Mr. Lewis, from the period that Governor Ramsey ceased to be an applicant, in consequence of the determination of the President to appoint a merchant, up to the time of his declaration that Mr. Lewis could never be appointed. Subsequently to this, as I have before stated, I supported Mr. Myers, and after he declined, I recommended Mr. Dale. I am thus minute, knowing that the omission of any fact, however trivial, would be laid hold of if possible and subjected to comment, without regard to fairness or candor.

Having arrived at the period of Mr. Lewis' appointment, which took place on the 8th or 9th of May, 1849, I proceed to show my agency in the appointment of George Read to the office of Weigher, dwelt on by him in his "narrative," at so much length and with so little truth. It cannot fail to be remarked that the object of this part of his "narrative," is to attribute to my influence the appointment of George Read; but it will be observed at the same time, that previous to the appointment of Read or any other person, he professes to have discovered, that I "*was then already in open or quasi hostility to both the State and National Administrations, although both were in the hands of the party to which I profess to belong;*" that in addition to this, it had become obvious to him, "*if all my demands for places for my friends were not complied with he would have to encounter my hostility when his name should come before the Senate;*" and further, that it "*had not escaped his attention that four of the persons on my list of special recommendations had, as members of the Legislature, voted for me when I was elected United States Senator.*" Notwithstanding, however, that he had discovered that I was unfaithful to the Whig party, determined to oppose his confirmation, and that I was improperly endeavoring to procure places for those who had voted for me as Senator, he was *constrained to oblige me* by appointing George Read, the man who, he asserts, was "nearest my heart"! Under such circumstances he could not overlook my anxious wishes! He knew that "*if all my demands were not complied with,*" I would oppose him. But notwithstanding this, in order to gratify me, he appointed a man who he knew, was unqualified, dishonest and likely to render him obnoxious to severe censure! How often does malignity overshoot its aim? That it has done so in this case will be shown by a narrative of the circumstances connected with the appointment of George Read, and Mr. Lewis' previous relations with and obligations to him.

On the 1st day of January, 1847, I had never seen George Read, nor did I know that there was such a person in existence. Shortly after the 1st of January, on the assembling of our Legislature, George W. South, whose personal acquaintance I then made, accompanied by George Read, came to Harrisburg. Mr. South, who brought me a letter from Wm. B. Reed, Esqr., introduced to me George Read as his friend. Thus began my acquaintance with Messrs. South and Read.*

During that winter a very animated contest for the nomination for Governor was carried on between my friends and those of General Irvin, in which Mr. South actively participated as a friend of mine. On the 9th of March, the Convention to nominate a candidate for Governor assembled at Harrisburg, where I was then attending to my duties as a member of the Legislature; and here I met George Read for the second time, in company with George W. South and William B. Reed. My intercourse with George Read was very slight on this occasion, and terminated with it until the 30th of August, 1848, when I again met him at Harrisburg, in the company of Mr. South, who was there as a delegate, representing Bucks County in the Convention which nominated Wm. F. Johnston, as a candidate for the office of Governor.

The business of the Convention having been finished, Messrs. South and Read called on me for a recommendation of the latter for the office of Bark Inspector of the City of Philadelphia, presenting at the same time a number of testimonials in his favor from gentlemen of high respectability, residing in the city. In pursuance of their request, I accompanied them to the Governor and united with Mr. South in recommending Read. From the representations of Mr. South and the testimonials which he produced, I did not entertain a doubt, either in relation to his character or qualifications for the office. Mr. Read, however, was not appointed, the policy which the Governor had determined to pursue, not permitting it at that time. Things stood thus until the assembling of the Electoral College, in December. Being at Harrisburg at that time, called thither by my

* It is possible that I had seen Mr. South once previously.

duties as Attorney General, I again met George Read, who came there in company with Mr. South to press his application for the inspectorship. On this occasion he brought with him numerous testimonials from gentlemen of standing and worth in the city, and amongst others, a letter to me from Wm. B. Reed, Esq., urging his appointment. At the solicitation of Mr. South, and accompanied by John Price Wetherill, Esqr., we called at the Executive Chamber to press the appointment of Mr. Read, an arrangement having been made between him and Mr. Yerkes, who had been a competitor for the same place; but if I recollect aright, we did not find the Governor in his room. We, however, placed Mr. Read's testimonials on file, and amongst them a letter signed by Messrs. South Wetherill and myself. I have mentioned the names of Messrs. Wm. B. Reed and John Price Wetherill for the purpose of showing that gentlemen residing in the same city with the applicant, and whose opportunities were much more ample than mine of becoming acquainted with his true character, were like myself imposed on;—for no one, who knows these gentlemen, will believe, for a moment, that either would knowingly recommend for a responsible office, a person so incompetent and so entirely destitute of every moral qualification as George Read is alleged to be. It is proper to state, that between the 30th of August, 1848, and the occasion last referred to, I had met Read several times, once at Mr. South's at a public meeting, and two or three times in Philadelphia.

About a month subsequently, on the 9th of January, 1849, the election of United States Senator took place at Harrisburg; and amongst the crowd assembled there were Messrs. George W. South and George Read, both professing to be friends of mine, nor have I any reason to doubt the sincerity of their professions. In the caucus which was held previously to the election, I received a large majority of the whole number of votes, my prominent competitors receiving but three votes each. I state this fact to show the gratuitous character of Mr. Lewis' insinuations, that four of the persons recommended to him by me for appointments, were members of the Legislature, and that it was to pay them for their votes, I had recommended them for office. Being thus the almost unanimous choice of the body, I had no occasion to resort to bribery, Mr. Lewis' favorite method of carrying a point; and when he made this insinuation, which would scarcely have entered into an honest man's mind, he would have done well to remember the forged circulars, recommending his confirmation by the Senate, as well as the corrupt arrangement by which he purchased the support of Lewis C. Levin for the office of Collector. The latter stated at a public meeting in Philadelphia, as is proved by the testimony of a number of witnesses, that before he would agree to support him for the office which he now holds, Mr. Lewis promised to give him the appointment of one-third of the officers in his gift. The extent of his participation in the forgery of the circulars, addressed to the Senate, will be seen by reference to the testimony taken by the Commissioner. But it is answer enough to the calumny insinuated by Mr. Lewis, that all four of the members referred to, came to Harrisburg my friends and did not need to be bribed into my support. One of these Mr. Lewis has since appointed to office himself—a proof, that if he believed his own insinuation, bribery is no very heinous offence in his eyes.

Between this period and that of the appointment of Mr. Lewis, in the May following, I saw George Read several times, and learned from him, that inasmuch as he had failed in his application to the Governor, he would apply for an appointment to the Collector. During this period I received from Mr. Read one or two letters, which at the time I did not doubt were written by himself—the fact of his inability to read or write not being known to me at that time.

Mr. Lewis was appointed, I think, on the 8th of May, 1849; and on the next day George Read came to Pottsville to solicit my aid in procuring for him the office of Weigher, bringing with him a letter from Mr. South, warmly urging me to recommend him. At first I declined, informing him that I had no claims upon Mr. Lewis, nor any influence with him. The latter statement Mr. Read combatted strongly, stating that *he knew* Mr. Lewis was prepared to do every thing that I would ask. Being exceedingly urgent, and appealing to me by every consideration likely to move me—by the friendship which he had manifested for me, first as a candidate for the nomination for Governor, and afterwards as a candidate for the United States Senate, and wearied by his importunities, I suffered my reluctance to be overcome, and gave him a letter, a copy of which is hereto annexed and marked B. This letter, the only one ever written by me to Mr. Lewis or any one else in favor of Read alone, was only a *conditional*, not an absolute recommendation, as will be seen by a reference to it.

This letter in favor of Read, was accompanied by another of the same date, addressed to Mr. Lewis, setting forth that I had received numerous communications from members of Congress, and influential gentlemen residing in various sections of the State, recommending certain persons, as the favorites of their respective counties and districts, and asking my good offices with him in their behalf; and that there were altogether some ten of these whose appointments would promote the interests of the Whig party in the interior. I then proceeded to indicate the salaries they would expect, ranging from $800 to $1500 per annum. The letter in favor of George Read refers to this, and states expressly, that I began by naming Read (I was not then in possession of the names of all the other applicants) "for whose appointment I am anxious, *provided* it could be made in pursuance of the proposition contained in my other letter of this date." This proposition was, that Read should be appointed, *provided* he would appoint the other applicants to whom I referred. See letter hereto annexed, and marked C.

These letters, as I have already stated, were the only ones ever addressed by me to Mr. Lewis, in which George Read's name was presented; nor did I ever write to any one else in his behalf alone; though *at the request* of Francis N. Buck, Esqr., I addressed him a letter containing the names which I had presented to Mr. Lewis in a personal interview to which I shall directly refer. George Read's name was mentioned amongst the others in the letter addressed to Mr. Buck. See the letter to Mr. Buck annexed and marked D.*

What now becomes of the assertion so continually reiterated in the "narrative" of Mr. Lewis, that Read's appointment was "nearest my heart," and that I was more anxious for it than for any other? It is false, like most of the rest.

But what I have stated is not the only proof of the falsity of Mr. Lewis' assertion. Two or three days after my letter in favor of Read was written, namely, on the 12th of May, I received a letter from Mr. Lewis, hereto annexed and marked I, inviting me to go to the city; but in the meantime having learned something of his true character from my friends, I addressed him a note, dated the 15th of May, hereto annexed and marked 2, requesting him to return both my former letters, or at least to consider the recommendations which they contained, withdrawn. That this letter was received by Mr. Lewis, I refer to his letter of the 17th of May, acknowledging the receipt of it. See letter No. 3, hereto annexed. This letter contains evidence of the determination of Mr. Lewis from the beginning to ascribe the appointment of George Read to me. His studied silence as to the contents of my letter of the 15th of

* Annexed to copy of this statement in hands of the President.

May, and his subsequent letter announcing to me the appointment of Mr. Read, and attributing it to my urgent solicitations, when he knew that I had withdrawn my recommendation in his favor, afford conclusive evidence of his predetermination to fix upon me the responsibility of his appointment.

A few days after the date of the last mentioned letter, I visited Philadelphia on business, and was but a little while there until Mr. Lewis called on me at my lodgings. At this time, it must be observed, I had not yet furnished him with the names of the applicants to whom I referred in my letters of the 10th of May; nor was it my intention to present them, after the notification of the withdrawal of my recommendations a few days previously. When he called, he spoke of the withdrawal of my recommendations, and expressed regret that I had done so. After conversing for some time, he requested me to furnish him with a list of the names of the persons I desired to be appointed. I at first declined; but as he insisted, stating at the same time, that it was his intention to satisfy the party throughout the State, as far as it was in his power, I consented, and gave him the names, which he took down himself. Taking down the names on a slip of paper, he inquired, as he did so, what was the lowest salary that would satisfy the applicants respectively, and as he learned it from me, he set it opposite their names. The names furnished are the same as those contained in my letter to Mr. Buck.

After he had thus procured the names of the persons, he asked me, if there was amongst them any individual about whose appointment I was particularly solicitous? I replied, that if I recommended them at all, I did it altogether, and did not desire the appointment of any one to the exclusion of any other; that I had promised several members of Congress, as well as influential Whigs in several of the counties, to recommend certain persons, the favorites of their respective districts and counties, and had pledged myself that they should all have alike the benefit of my recommendation, whether that was much or little. He, however, insisted on knowing whether any one of them was a particular personal friend, and recommended on my own account. I finally indicated Robert W. McSherry as being the only one recommended on my own account; but at the same time, I repeated, that I did not desire his appointment at the expense of that of any other. Mr. Lewis, however, marked a name; but in so doing made a mistake, as I afterwards inferred from his letter, dated the 30th of May, announcing to me the appointment of Henry J. Schreiner, in which he states, "*this is the gentleman in whom I understood you to feel a particular personal interest.*" This proves that Mr. Lewis knew his assertion, that I felt greater anxiety for the appointment of George Read than any other person, to be false. He gives the lie to it under his own hand.

But I have not yet done with the evidence of Mr. Lewis' falsehoods in relation to my agency in the appointment of George Read. In my letter to him, introducing Robert W. McSherry, and reiterating my recommendation of him, I state expressly, that he "is the gentleman of whom I *spoke* as the only one I had named on my own account." See letter hereto annexed, marked F, and put in evidence by Mr. Lewis himself.

After withdrawing my recommendation of Read and others, on the 15th of May, five or six days after Mr. Lewis' appointment, I never addressed him another word in favor of George Read; nor in the only interview which I had with him was Mr. Read's name mentioned, except on the occasion of furnishing the list of names to which I have before referred. Nor in correspondence with any one else, did I ever refer to Read, except generally as one of those whom I had first recommended. Indeed, after the withdrawal of my recommendation, it was not my intention to do any thing further in the matter; nor should I ever have departed from my determination in that respect, even to furnish the names, had it not been for the request of Mr. Lewis, and the urgent solicitation of friends of my own, to whom I was in some sort pledged to recommend certain persons to be indicated by them, and of mutual friends of Mr. Lewis and myself, who were anxious that there should be no misunderstanding between us, and who expressed themselves confident that Mr. Lewis would appoint all whom I had named. Of this number was Mr. Buck, at whose request I addressed him the letter hereto annexed. Thus it is apparent, that instead of manifesting more solicitude for the appointment of George Read, than for that of any other person, I manifested none, except what is to be gathered from a letter, but little urgent in its general import, and which is, in its terms, strictly *conditional*, viz., on the appointment of all the others whom I had recommended. I might have been more urgent for his appointment; for at that time I knew nothing to his prejudice. I thought, however, that I could discover on the part of Mr. Lewis a disposition to induce me to urge upon him the appointment of Mr. Read for some sinister purpose; therefore it was, that notwithstanding solicitations of the most pressing kind on the part of South,* Weaver, and Levin, I refused any active participation in their efforts in his behalf. I

* See South's letter marked Y.

know that he has been induced by an unscrupulous man to ascribe his appointment to me; but the means by which it was procured is disclosed by George W. South, *one of Mr. Lewis' witnesses*, in his testimony before the Commissioner. It is as follows:

Q. Did you and the other friends of Mr. Read obtain the approval of the authorities at Washington by anticipation before Mr. Lewis would make the appointment?

A. On the Thursday or Friday before Mr. Read's appointment, I was in the City, and called to see Mr. Lewis at the Custom House, to ascertain, if possible, if he intended Mr. Read to that post or not. I found Mr. Lewis in a little different mood from a few days before. He rather faltered upon the subject of appointing Mr. Read, for I supposed he was going to throw him overboard. I inquired the cause of his changing his mind. He said the *Ultra Whig party* had made a dead set at him, that he, Read, *had formerly been a Democrat*. Mr. Lewis added that *he had every disposition to accommodate Mr. Cooper and myself.* I went home to the country feeling very uncertain as to whether Read would be appointed or not.

On Sunday morning I received a message from Philadelphia, stating that Mr. David Winebrener and George J. Weaver, desired particularly to see me upon that subject. I came to town immediately, and saw Mr. Winebrener and Mr. W.

Q. Did Mr. Lewis agree to appoint him until after you should apply to the authorities at Washington?

A. *No, sir.*

Q. Did you so apply?

A. *Yes, sir, we did.*

Q. Was the appointment by anticipation?

A. *It was by the Sec. of the Treas'y, Mr. Meredith.*

Q. Was this approval communicated to Mr. Lewis?

A. *It was.*

Q. Was he afterwards appointed?

A. *He was.*

* * * * * * *

Q. At whose request did you visit the Sec. of the Treas'y in relation to Read's appointment?

A. *I understood it to be at Mr. Lewis' request.*

Q. Who called upon Mr. Meredith with you?

A. Mr. David Winebrener, Mr. George Weaver.

Q. Was Mr. Levin with you?

A. No, sir, not on that occasion.

Q. Did he accompany you at any visit to any functionary in Washington, in relation to Read's appointment?

A. Mr. Levin accompanied Mr. Weaver, Mr. Winebrenner, Mr. Dall and myself on a visit to Mr. Clayton, to the Sec. of War, Mr. Crawford, Mr. Preston, in relation to the appointment of Geo. Read. *Mr. Levin spoke of him, and it was to advise his appointment. He was appointed immediately on our return, which was a day or two after.*

Q. Why, sir, was it deemed necessary that the consent of Mr. Meredith to the appointment of Read should be had before the appointment was made?

A. *Mr. Lewis said that clamors had been raised as to Read's politics,* and he did not wish to send his name down *until he knew whether Mr. Meredith would confirm it or not.*

*   *   *   *   *

Q. Did Mr. Cooper take any other part in this matter than to write the two letters which you have before spoken of?

A. *Never to my knowledge.*

In the interim, between the time Mr. Lewis received his appointment and the appointment of Read, there were frequent givings out that he could not be appointed; at one time, it was stated that Mr. Morris was to be appointed; at another, Mr. Murray; and all this, I believed then, and believe still, was to induce me to a more active interference in Mr. Read's behalf. In the meantime, as I have already stated, those immediately interested in his appointment, made extraordinary efforts to secure my active co-operation in bringing it about. But they used other means far more efficacious with Mr. Lewis, than any interference of mine could have been. It is, however, believed by those best acquainted with the previous relations existing between Lewis and Read, that the appointment of the latter had been determined from the beginning.

To show the intense anxiety of Messrs. South, Weaver, Levin, and other confidential friends of Mr. Lewis, for the appointment of George Read, it is only necessary to notice the extraordinary exertions in his behalf. Messrs. South, Weaver and others visited Washington, where they were joined by Mr. Levin, who united with them in obtaining the confirmation of his appointment by the Secretary of the Treasury before it was made by the Collector; thus procuring a kind of *quasi* order from the Secretary in his favor. I do not desire to be understood, that Mr. Meredith directed his appointment to be made; but that his consent, to confirm it, was procured beforehand. All this was done with the consent and approval of Mr. Lewis. See South's testimony already referred to.

Shortly before the appointment of Read, on one occasion, I arrived in Philadelphia at night, and had scarcely got to my room at the hotel, when I was waited on by Levin, Weaver and Read, who requested me to accompany them to see Mr. Lewis at his own house, in order to urge Read's appointment. I, however, declined either to see Mr. Lewis or to urge the appointment of Mr. Read, on any other condition than that proposed to Mr. Lewis in the interview already referred to, though most earnestly importuned to do so, by all three of the gentlemen. After a long continued but fruitless effort to induce me to change my determination and recommend Mr. Read, Mr. Levin went to see Mr. Lewis, requesting me not to go to bed, (it was then eleven o'clock on Sunday night,) until his return. He soon came back, and informed me that Mr. Lewis was still up, and would be glad to see me. Strong appeals were made by the whole party, to induce me to go with them; but as I continued to refuse, Messrs. Weaver and Read departed alone. In the course of an hour they returned, with a proposition from Mr. Lewis to appoint Messrs. Read, Robb and Nicholas Thorne, and that he would stay up, although it was then past midnight, in order to give me an opportunity to signify to him my acceptance of this offer. Wearied by the importunities of Weaver and Read, and irritated by the presumption of the former, who had promised Mr. Lewis that I should accept his proposition, I terminated the interview by an emphatic rejection, and in terms which even the impudent perseverance of these men understood to be conclusive. It is but just to Mr. Levin to state, that on this occasion he was less importunate than his fellows. Such were the pains taken by the friends of Mr. Lewis, and so great was his own anxiety to procure my recommendation of Read!

That it was determined in advance to charge this appointment to me, is evident from the terms in which it was announced by Mr. Lewis in his letter of the 30th of May, of which he was careful enough to preserve a copy for future use. This letter sets forth, "that, in consequence of the urgency with which I had advocated the appointment of George Read, Esq., to the highly responsible post of Weigher, he had that day appointed him," &c. And in the late proceeding before the Commissioner at Philadelphia, Mr. Lewis produced a copy of this letter, and annexed it to the record, to prove my anxiety in behalf of Read! (See letter.)*

There is quite too much forecast in announcing to me the appointment, in setting forth the reasons for it, and preserving a copy, not to afford evidence of a design of some kind. It would, perhaps, be profitable to inquire whether he announced any other appointment in similar terms, and preserved a copy of the letter.

But, it may be asked, if Mr. Lewis himself was anxious for the appointment of George Read, and determined to make it, why he required so much solicitation before he consented to it? Several reasons might be furnished. *First*, others desired his appointment, and might be obliged and gratified by his making it, if he withheld from them his determination to do it on his own account. *Secondly*, and more probably, his former connection with George Read in cer-

* Marked F.

tain perilous circumstances rendered it necessary that he should appoint him, in order to avoid disagreeable, if not dangerous disclosures; and being under such necessity, and aware of his lack of qualifications, morally and otherwise, he was anxious for reasons to justify himself in making the appointment in the strength and quality of his recommendations. Hence the desire of his friends, South, Weaver, and Levin, acting by his request, to procure my more active interference in his behalf; and hence, too, his request, that a *quasi* order from the Secretary of the Treasury, in the shape of a confirmation, should be procured in advance. The greatest anxiety, any where existing for this appointment, was evidently on the part of Lewis and South.*

That Mr. Lewis was perfectly acquainted with George Read, is manifest from the fact that they were concerned together at Harrisburg, in procuring the passage of the relief law, and that they were afterwards examined before the same committee, touching the bribery and fraud by which it was then believed, and is still believed, the passage of the law was effected. Read, in this matter, it is evident from the testimony taken in the case, was the instrument of worse men. Who these were, may be guessed by those who will take the trouble to examine the report of the Committee, and the testimony on which it was based.

But it is idle for Mr. Lewis to attribute the appointment of George Read to my influence; and it is an answer to all that has been said, that knowing him when he was appointed, and knowing the gross improprieties of which he has since been guilty, he still retains him in office. To save himself from the odium which is accumulating around, and threatening to overwhelm him, it is probable he would have removed him long ago, but for the fear, that by so doing, "a worse thing might come upon him." Poor man! Even the base and wicked may enlist our pity; and in retaining Read in office, if we could be made aware of his inward conflict between fear and interest, the intensest of all the feelings which are left to him, except, perhaps, vindictiveness, he would be the object of our commiseration as much as of our scorn.

That I recommended George Read with too little caution, as was done by others as well as myself, I am ready to admit. But at the time I did so I was unaware that he lacked either qualifications or integrity. He had been politically my friend, and I was grateful, as I ever am, to those who have been so. I heard of his appointment without dissatisfaction, and regretted afterwards when I learned

* See letter marked Y.

that I had been deceived in his character, as Mr. Meredith appears to have been, when he confirmed his appointment.

There are many other circumstances which I have not noticed, all going to show, that Mr. Lewis knew his statements relative to my agency in George Read's appointment to be untrue; but I omit them for the present; and only repeat, that his conduct, in retaining this man in office, after the numerous disclosures in regard to his conduct, show that they are bound together in a knot of circumstances which Mr. Lewis cannot untie and dare not cut. One other thing is certain, viz. that Read is not retained in office through any regard on the part of Lewis for me.

The next charge preferred against me by Mr. Lewis, is, that I did not act with candor in avowing what course I intended to pursue in relation to his nomination; that to some I declared I would support it, to others that I would oppose it, and to a third class that I had not made up my mind as to the course which I should pursue. This charge is wilfully false. To no human being did I ever say I would support his nomination; nor did I declare until near the assembling of Congress in December, 1849, that I had made up my mind definitely to oppose it—except, perhaps, on two or three occasions, when irritated by the report of invidious and disparaging remarks, made in relation to me by Mr. Lewis. When I did make up my mind, his own friends were the first informed of it. Being in Philadelphia, in November, '49, Mr. Levin came to see me at my lodgings, and in the course of conversation on the subject, I informed him that it was my determination to oppose his confirmation. He used various arguments and made several offers, then and subsequently, to induce me to change my purpose. Amongst other things he offered in the name of Mr. Lewis, as soon as the latter should be confirmed, to turn out all the Democrats then remaining in office under him, and to appoint my friends in their places. This offer, so far as it related to the turning out of the Democrats and replacing them with Whigs, he renewed at my room in Washington, after the assembling of Congress in December, 1849, in the presence of Messrs. Ogle and Pitman, and Lieut. Parke of the Army. See letter of the two former gentlemen hereto annexed and marked G. Whilst thus engaged in endeavoring to make me believe, that it was the intention of Mr. Lewis to remove the Democrats holding places under him, as soon as he should be confirmed, he was laboring with Democratic Senators and others to create the belief that it was his determination to retain them. These offers and declarations on the part of

Mr. Levin would be unimportant, were it not known that he acted as the confidential agent of Mr. Lewis, in matters touching the confirmation of his nomination, and that he was interested in it so far, according to his own declarations publicly made, that it had been agreed between him and Mr. Lewis, previous to his embarking in the support of the latter, that he should have the naming of *one-third* of the Custom House subordinates. And not only did he act as agent himself, but had the power, at least exercised it, of appointing sub-agents, to attend to such portions of the work as he had not time to perform himself, and which Mr. Lewis ratified by paying them on Mr. Levin's order to that effect. When this is denied I will furnish evidence to prove it.

After the assembling of Congress, I was repeatedly called on by Mr. Levin, not to learn my determination in relation to Mr. Lewis, but to urge and intreat me to change it. I never had but one answer for him, namely, that my mind was made up and that I would oppose his confirmation. When he discovered that my determination was irrevocable he ceased his attempt to change it, but begged that I should take no steps to the prejudice of Mr. Lewis with the Senators until I should inform him I was about to do so. To this I consented, inasmuch as the nomination had not then been sent to the Senate. A day or two after it was sent in, I informed him that I would call it up for action as soon as possible; and I did, in company with my colleague, call upon the Committee of Commerce and urge them to report; and this we continued to do weekly, for nearly eight months, before a report could be procured. In the meantime, on every occasion, I expressed my opposition to his confirmation; and I venture to say that there was not a member of either House, who ever heard me express myself doubtfully or hesitatingly on the subject.

Previously to this, George W. South visited Washington for the purpose of endeavoring to secure my vote for the confirmation of Mr. Lewis. His efforts to accomplish his object were zealous and persevering; but I did not leave him a moment in doubt as to my course. I told him at once, in the most decisive terms, that his efforts must be fruitless. This charge, that I was not frank, open and decided, is the last which I supposed would be preferred against me in this matter; for I repeat here, that no human being, at any time, ever heard me say I would vote for his confirmation; and from the early part of January, my opposition, was open, notorious, consistent and known to all. To the particular friends of Mr. Lewis it had been known long before.

After the failure of Mr. South's attempt to induce me to vote for Mr. Lewis, I was visited several times by another gentleman with the like object; but it is due to truth to say that his conduct on the occasion was entirely unexceptionable and proper. He made no propositions, stating only that he was a friend of Mr. Lewis, and anxious for his confirmation; that he thought if we could meet, Mr. Lewis could free himself from the charges which had been preferred against him, and explain such portions of his conduct as I deemed objectionable. My answer to him was the same as to Mr. South; and I have no doubt he will say, that the expression of my opposition was frank and prompt, and that I informed him, it was founded not only on the injustice of his conduct towards myself and my friends, but also on charges of dishonesty as a man, which leaving the former out of view, ought not to be overlooked or disregarded. He said in reply, the former might be remedied; and that he felt confident the latter was groundless and might be explained. He likewise stated that Mr. Lewis was in the city and anxious to see me, provided I would consent. I did so and the interview took place the same evening. or the evening following. Mr. Lewis' version of what occurred, having been made public through the medium of his "narrative," my lips, closed until now, are unsealed; and it will be seen whose account savors most of the truth. There was no witness present; and both he and I must rely upon the character which we have respectively earned for veracity and honesty, and upon the intrinsic marks of truth or falsehood which every narrative of facts contains, to a greater or less extent, in itself.

When Mr. Lewis called on me several members of my family were present, but on an intimation from him that he desired to see me alone, they withdrew. He commenced the conversation by saying he regretted the unfriendly attitude which we occupied towards each other; that, he had no doubt, pretended friends on both sides, had been instrumental in producing estrangement and misunderstanding between us; that I had been misrepresented to him, and he supposed he had been misrepresented to me. I said in reply, that I had no doubt that this was to some extent the case. He then went on to say, that from the position in which things stood, in relation to his confirmation, there was no hope of correcting the misunderstanding which existed, except through an unreserved and frank communication of what I required on my part, and what he was willing to concede on his; and that such interchange of communication, free and full as it ought to be, if any thing were to be accomplished by it, involved the necessity of trusting each other. In the circumstances in which we are placed, said he, you will not tell me what you require of me, unless you can confide in my honor, that what is said here will never be repeated elsewhere; nor would I be willing to state, what I might be prepared to concede, if I could not trust to your honor, not to use it to my prejudice in the Senate. Sir, continued he, rising from his seat and traversing the room, I have considered this subject, and am willing to trust you, if you will 'trust me; adding in a peculiar tone, I think Mr. Cooper, that notwithstanding Girard Bank stories, you have never heard my personal veracity or honor impeached. To this I made an evasive reply, not desiring to offend or wound him; but after some remarks, rather general in their character, it was mutually agreed that the subjects of the conversation should never be repeated.

But as Mr. Lewis has seen fit to violate an express understanding, the articles of which were proposed by himself, by publishing a statement of what took place at the interview, which is false in every material particular, I feel absolved from any further obligation to preserve silence. I shall therefore proceed to state exactly what he proposed and I accepted, as well as what I proposed and he rejected.

In the first place, he proposed to do justice to my friends, that is to appoint those whom I had originally recommended, with the exception of one who had become addicted to habits of intemperance;* and in his place he agreed to appoint some other person whom I was to name. And on my suggesting that one of those whom I had recommended had been since elected to a lucrative office, and that one or two of the others had received appointments elsewhere, it was agreed I should name an equal number in their place. Afterwards, however, Mr. Lewis suggested, that if I had no objection, he would prefer that the persons to be appointed should be named by my friends, remarking that something was due to consistency on his part; and that as he had previously declared, under the influence of irritated feelings, that he would appoint nobody on my recommendation, he would be glad the applications should be made by others. I replied that I had no objection; that my object was to secure situations for good and deserving men, and I cared not through whose immediate

* This was long after the appointment of George Reed.

agency they obtained them ; that at any rate they were not individuals of my own selection, nor recommended as such in the beginning, and that being assured of their appointment I was quite willing they should be presented by others.

This being concluded, Mr. Lewis then aked me, what more I would demand? I answered, that I would expect the printing patronage of his office to be distributed amongst all the Whig papers of the city, and not confined to the Sun and North American; and that he must settle the difficulty with Harris & Co., relative to the stock transaction which he had had with them. At this proposition he became excited, but soon recovered his composure. At first he demurred to the whole of it; but after a little conversation agreed to so much of it as related to the distribution of the patronage, remarking, however, that it would be a "bitter pill" to aid the "News," which, he said, had always been hostile to him.

To the proposition to settle with Harris & Co., he continued to object strenuously. He declared the claim was dishonest, and asked me what interest I had in the matter? I answered none; that I had never seen Mr. Harris, or any body connected with him; but as I had given that transaction as a principal reason of my opposition to him, I could not support his nomination until he relieved himself from the odium in which it involved him. I told him that I had a statement of the facts, and that it placed his conduct in a very unfavorable light, implicating his honor as a gentleman, and his integrity as a man of business. At this point he became agitated, walking up and down the room in a good deal of excitement. Finally stopping, he said, Mr. Cooper, I see you wish to drive a hard bargain with me; but do you think it right to insist that I should pay a dishonest claim? I answered, No; that if he would satisfy me it was unfounded, or get from Mr. Harris any thing to show that it had been settled, so that I could justify myself in supporting his nomination, I would do it.

He asked me to show him the statement; which I declined, but gave him the substance of it. I declined to show it to him, because it was in the handwriting of a gentleman, who did not wish to be implicated; and with whose handwriting I presumed he was acquainted. He made an attempt at explanation, but it was not satisfactory. After some conversation touching his chances of confirmation, the interview terminated, with a promise on his part to see me again in relation to the transaction in question.

As to his statements that, I said his character was above my reach, and that I would oppose his confirmation on political grounds alone; that I could barter my votes to secure his rejection, and that he said to me such a course on my part would be derogatory to my character, and never be countenanced by the Senate, these all and each are false in every particular. Not a word of the kind was said, either by him or me. These statements bear the impress of falsehood on their face; and so, he seemed to think himself, when he states in his "narrative," "should this statement of the conversation appear incredible, the doubt will vanish, when it is known that the Senator addressed a letter to a member of Congress, to be used in promoting my nomination to the office of Collector, on the same day that he furnished the same member with a letter equally strong in favor of another applicant for the same place, to be used in the like manner." This last falsehood, resorted to to help out another as gross, has been already disproved. I again challenge the production of the last mentioned letter. Mr. Lewis has published every letter which I have ever addressed to him, as well as several which I have addressed to other persons, whose notions of propriety permitted them to furnish him with copies, whenever the letters could be, by distortion or falsehood, made to subserve his purposes. If the letters in question would promote his object, they would have been produced, as well as my letter of the 15th of May, 1849, (referred to in his of the 17th,) withdrawing my recommendations of Read and others. It will give the lie direct to Lewis and his friend and coadjutor, Levin.

The "narrative" next proceeds to state, that the day after our interview, I intimated to a third party that if he, Lewis, would support the "Daily News," my objections would be removed; and that I subsequently informed "a distinguished Democratic Senator, that he had promised to remove all the Democrats holding places under him, and give to me the choice of their successors; that I informed Whig Senators that he had pledged himself to retain the Democrats, and Democratic Senators that he had pledged himself to turn them out in the event of his confirmation."

This is totally untrue. I never intimated to any body that I would be satisfied with his support of the "Daily News:" nor did I ever inform any Democratic Senator, distinguished or otherwise, that he had proposed to remove his Democratic subordinates, and fill their places with Whigs of my selection. Of what he proposed at our interview, I never spoke to any one, Whig or Democrat.

That I stated frequently, both to Whigs and Democrats, in the Senate and out of it, that he had declared to the Whigs he would remove the Democrats as soon as he was confirmed, while at the same time he was pledging himself to the Democrats, through the medium of his agents, to retain them, I do not deny. That he declared to the Whigs he would remove the Democrats as soon as he was confirmed, I refer to the affidavit of Mathias Meyers, Esq., hereto annexed, and marked H.* That his agent, Lewis C. Levin, did the same, the certificate of Messrs. Ogle and Pitman, already referred to, will prove.

Afterwards, in the Senate, pending the question of his confirmation, to procure Democratic votes, he authorized Mr. Clarke, one of the Senators from Rhode Island, to pledge him not to remove the Democrats. To procure the votes of the Whig members, he relied upon circulars, how got up and through whose agency, I refer to the testimony taken before Mr. Dunlevy.

Another charge contained in Mr. Lewis' "narrative," is, that large sums of money were wagered on his defeat by my friends, and the insinuation is palpable, that it was done at my suggestion. The insinuation is gratuitous, and entirely false. That considerable sums were wagered by different individuals, I believe is true; but I presume there was as much wagered for as against his confirmation. George Read, and others of his subordinates, betted freely, and it is proved that they were generally, if not always, the challengers; and Mr. Lewis himself authorized bets to be made that he would be confirmed; and one such at least was made. In possession of the means of securing recommendations at pleasure, he felt that there was little risk of betting his money. See affidavit of Lane Schofield hereto annexed, and marked I. Mr. Lewis made an affidavit contradicting that of Schofield; but as he was swearing in his own cause, to win both his money and his office, little credit will be attached to it.

The "narrative" next proceeds to state, that I made every effort to prejudice the Committee of Commerce against him, and that after his nomination had been eight months before it, and it had finally agreed upon a unanimous report in his favor, he has reason to believe that I brought new charges to its notice, demanded a reconsideration, which was granted, and that the result was a re-affirmation on the part of the Committee. This, too, is untrue, as the Committee will testify. I preferred to it no new charges; I asked no reconsideration, and none was ever had.

* Annexed to the copy of this statement in the hands of the President.

Passing over a page or two of very gross abuse relative to my opposition to him in the Senate, he comes to speak of what followed the presentation of the testimony taken before the Mayor. He says, "the garbage thus collected was laid by Mr. Cooper before the Senate, and of course disgusted every member but one, who finding my confirmation certain, asked for a week's further delay, which was refused"! This is not true. I asked for no delay; but being ill, a Democratic Senator moved a postponement of the subject until the next day, which prevailed. At this time the testimony taken in Philadelphia had not been presented; and when it was afterwards presented, the matter was disposed of on the same day. After the motion to postpone had been made, I was absent from the Senate, for perhaps a week, confined to my bed, during the whole of the time by serious indisposition; and after I became better, and returned to the Senate, several days elapsed before it again went into executive session, though I was there in attendance, anxious to resume and settle the question. This much by way of exposing another of his falsehoods.

I pass over the pardonable display of Mr. Lewis' vanity, in announcing, that the fact of his confirmation was conveyed to him "by the venerable statesman and patriot whose fame is expanded over both hemispheres, and with whom, thirty-six years before, he traversed the ocean when he went on the mission of peace." Men who have forfeited their right to associate with respectable people, generally make much case of an occasional notice at their hands, even though it should be purely accidental.

I also pass by the fact, which he parades with a good deal of ostentation, that on his return from Washington to Philadelphia, after his confirmation, he "was received with unexpected and distinguished honor," by the Tide-waiters and other Custom House officials, as well as of the invitation, extended to him, to partake of a public dinner. A man's character is at a low ebb when it is necessary to sustain it by testimony like this. A mandate to that effect, issued by George Read, or any other confidential convenient friend, to whom he might whisper a wish to that effect, would assemble the Tide-waiters to do him "honor;" and a hint to those whose interest it is to stand well with the Collector, would procure him an invitation to dinner.

That I have done any thing to annoy him since his confirmation, as he alleges, or had any thing to do in getting up the charges lately prefered against him, I utterly deny. After the investigation had been ordered, I wrote to, as well as consulted with Mr. Corwin, as to the manner in which it should be conducted; and when it was likely to fail from the limitation of the scope of the inquiry, as settled by the instructions of Mr. Corwin to the Commissioner, I interfered at the request of numerous citizens of Philadelphia, to have them enlarged, and for this purpose wrote to the President. That my suggestions, in this respect, were proper, is proved by the fact that they were almost entirely adopted by the President. These were the only only acts of mine, subsequent to his confirmation, which has tended to place Mr. Lewis in the disagreeable attitude in which he now stands, and which has called forth the flood of impotent malice with which his "narrative" overflows. The charges against him were preferred, without prompting by men whose character is above the reach of detraction; and that he knows this, is manifest enough from the fact that he has not dared to assail them. He has, however, craftily endeavored to create the impression that he is the victim of persecution, excited by Mr. Gibbons and myself. But if this were as true as it is false, it would afford no justification for the forgery and fraud by which the confirmation of his nomination was secured; nor for the retention in office of the agents through whose instrumentality it was effected His long acquaintance, intimate connection, and confidential relations with George Read, in circumstances of peril to their reputation, and the eminent services which he has received at the hands of the latter, may account for his attachment to him: but do not excuse him, as a public officer, for retaining him in a place, the duties of which he cannot perform. Gratitude is an ennobling virtue, and the treasury of Mr. Lewis being well nigh bankrupt, in this respect, he should have credit for it; but he would be entitled to greater credit were he to display his gratitude at his own expense instead of that of the public.

I am now approaching the conclusion of this long "narrative" of calumnies, which is pervaded by a studied attempt to induce the belief that my opposition to his confirmation was the result of disappointment, and without any other "imaginable motive." A brief statement will show whether my opposition was groundless or not.

One of my reasons for opposing the confirmation of his nomination was his want of any fixed political principles, or identification with either of the great parties of the country. In his political conduct he resembles those camp-followers and plunderers, who travel in the wake of armies, and shout for the victors, in order to share the spoils. Attached to no standard, exposed to no danger in the combat, but first upon the field when the battle is won, he is prepared to appropriate the fruits of the victory. Few persons *knew* Mr. Lewis as a Whig, though some alleged that he was one at heart. Few knew him as a Democrat, though many believed him to be so. The scales of the balance he managed to keep pretty even; and possessing much craft, no shame, and great unscrupulousness, he generally managed to get more or less from the party in power. Still, as he had been nominated by a Whig President, and was advocated by some worthy men, had his character been otherwise tolerably free from reproach, and his conduct as an officer unexceptionable, I would probably have voted for him, though certainly with reluctance. This was not the case, as the following will prove.

Sometime in the winter of 1845, I think it was, Mr. Lewis being engaged in stock transactions, had contracted to deliver to some person or persons, 865 shares of the stock of the Philadelphia, Wilmington and Baltimore Rail Road Company. When the time for the delivery of the stock approached, he found himself unable to comply with his agreement, not having the stock, and not being able to procure it. On making known his situation to his friends, it was suggested that he might probably procure it from Messrs. Harris and Co., brokers in the City of Philadelphia, and gentlemen of great respectability and liberality, who were in possession of the principal part of the stock. He accordingly applied to them; and by the urgent intercession of friends, procured a loan of the stock—865 shares, on which he paid $28 or $29, or a gross sum amounting to about that much per share, which was to be repaid to him, when the stock should be returned. For its return a time was fixed; but when it arrived, he was unable to comply with his contract, and was in great distress, inasmuch as a failure involved his expulsion from the Board of Brokers, of which he was a member, if the rules should be enforced. In this emergency his friends were again appealed to, and amongst others he called on Charles Henry Fisher, Esqr., and represented to him the state of his affairs, begging him to call on Messrs. Harris & Co., and use his influence to induce them to *sell* to him the stock which he had borrowed and was unable to return. The selling price of the stock was then about $40 per share, and was principally in the hands of these gentlemen. Mr. Fisher, in pursuance of the request of Mr. Lewis, called on them and represented his condition, urging them to sell him the stock. They desired to see Mr. Lewis, who accordingly waited on them. At the interview he informed them, that though his means was ample, they consisted principally in mortgages and real estate, which were not presently available. After some conversation, they agreed to sell him the stock at $39 per share, a dollar below the selling price; and as he had not the money to pay the cash for it, they charged him on their books with the difference between $29, the amount which he had advanced, per share, when he obtained the loan, and $39, the amount per share which he had agreed to pay—some $8000 or $9000—Mr. Lewis expressing great satisfaction at the arrangement.

Some two or three months afterwards, Harris & Co., settling up their transactions in the stock of the Philadelphia, Wilmington and Baltimore Rail Road Company, sent Mr. Lewis their account, which he then refused, and still refuses to pay. By an act of the Legislature of Pennsylvania, all sales and transactions of stock in any corporation or company, payable more than five days after date, are declared void, and are consequently irrecoverable by law. Of this act Mr. Lewis took advantage, and defrauded his benefactors, who had generously befriended him in the hour of his need, trusting to his honor for payment. This debt still remains unpaid. For a fuller and more particular history of this transaction, see depositions of Joseph C. Harris and Charles Henry Fisher, Esqrs., hereto annexed and marked J.*

This is a part of the testimony taken before the Mayor of Philadelphia, to disprove which, Mr. Lewis declares in his "narrative" it "was deemed unnecessary, that a single witness should be called," so signal, says he, "was Mr. Cooper's failure to blacken my character." If this did not blacken it, it must be because it was too black before to take a deeper hue.

Regarding this most dishonorable transaction,.as too trifling for notice, as Mr. Lewis declares it to be, some estimate may be formed of his notions of propriety and fair dealing. Most men would regard this transaction as infamous; Mr. Lewis, however, is of a different opinion!

But this is not the only transaction in which Mr. Lewis' disposition to help himself at the expense of those who have been his benefactors, is exhibited. In 1831 or 1832, Messrs. Edward D. Whitney and William Whitney were engaged, if I mistake not, in carrying on the business of commission merchants in the city of New York. Meeting with Mr. Lewis about this time, he prevailed on them to go to Philadelphia and open a commission house in that city, in which Mr. Lewis was to be a partner. By the agreement entered

* Annexed to the copy of this statement in possession of the President.

into between them, Mr. Lewis was to furnish the capital, the Whitneys to conduct the business, under the style of Lewis and Whitney. Lewis was to furnish $60,000 in money, $40,000 of which was to be paid immediately on the commencement of the business, and the balance in the course of the year. He, however, failed to do this, furnishing only about $2500, and at the end of the year being in debt to the firm about $2000; at the end of the second year about $7000; and at the dissolution of the firm, which took place, I think, in the third year, he was in debt to it something above $19,000. In the meantime his conduct was anything but proper, frequently disposing of the paper of the house in stock and other speculations, for his immediate benefit, at ruinous discounts, which he charged to the firm.

Sometime after this, Mr. Lewis became embarrassed, and applied for means to relieve himself to his brother John Lewis, a man of large wealth, who resided in London. The latter agreed to advance him 5000 pounds sterling, provided he could procure the certificate of Charles Chauncey, Esqr., that such sum would pay his debts and set him afloat again. His indebtedness was considerable to other persons, besides the Whitneys, to whom he owed over $19,000 on account of the partnership debt above stated; and in addition to this, the price of 500 shares of the stock of the Girard Bank, purchased by him at $70 per share.

Under these circumstances he called on the Messrs. Whitney, and offered to give them his notes, endorsed by his brother-in-law, Thomas C. Rockhill, Esqr., a man of considerable wealth, for the $19,000, provided they would discharge him from *legal liability* to pay for the stock, offering to return them 400 shares, the other 100, according to my recollection of the testimony, having been disposed of—at any rate, the sum for which he asked a release amounted to about $8,000. This sum they were to trust to his honor to pay when he became able. This he pledged himself he would do. They hesitated. He reasoned with them, showing them that it would be to their advantage, under any circumstances, to accept his proposition; that it would ensure to them the payment of the larger sum at all events, and enable him in all probability, soon to pay the others. He stated, that unless he was relieved from his obligation to pay for the stock, he could not procure the certificate of Mr. Chauncey, and consequently could not get the five thousand pounds promised him by his brother. Moved by his distress, and the threats which he made to destroy himself, before he would encounter the exposure and ruin which awaited him, they finally consented, took his notes endorsed by Mr. Rockhill for the $19,000, and his word of honor to pay the balance, due on the stock, when he should become able, and gave him a receipt in full, on the back of his account. He obtained the money from his brother, and being cashier of the Girard Bank, soon retrieved his circumstances. Afterwards, when the condition of the parties had changed, the Messrs. Whitneys having become poor, and Mr. Lewis rich, they called on him for the money; but their demands were treated with contempt, sometimes with insult and outrage. The debt remains unpaid to this day, Mr. Lewis sheltering himself behind the fact, that in preparing his schedule, when he took the benefit of the bankrupt law, Mr. Edward D. Whitney omitted to state this debt amongst his assets. But it is answer enough, that it was not a legal demand, which could be enforced at law. Stating these facts from memory, I may not have done it with entire accuracy. Substantially, however, the facts are as I have set them forth. If I have erred, it is in Mr. Lewis' favor. See depositions of Edward D. and William Whitney, and letters of Messrs. Whitney and Lewis, which I will procure, annexed marked K.* In these cases, Mr. Lewis' gratitude does not shine forth so conspicuously as in that of George Read. But some allowance must be made for the difference, on the score of congeniality between him and the latter.

So much for his conduct previously to his appointment; a word now as to his actions since in the discharge of the duties of his office.

James S. Wallace, Editor of the Philadelphia Sun, was appointed in June or July, 1849, an Inspector of Customs by Mr. Lewis, at a salary of $3 per day, amounting to $1095 per annum, and during that time has performed no services, as was proved by a number of witnesses examined before the Mayor of Philadelphia in September last. In November, 1849, I met Mr. Wallace in Philadelphia, after he had been some five months in office, and he then told me, he had performed no services, and never had been required to perform any. Yet his account is made out every month, sworn to, certified by the Surveyor, Mr. Norris, and transmitted to the Treasury Department by Mr. Lewis. The bill for services rendered by the Inspectors are printed, and require the duties which are performed to be particularized. When these officers do nothing, they are set down as

* Annexed to the copy of this statement with the President.

being so many days "in aid of customs;" when at work, so many days in charge of ship B. or brig A., as the case may be.

Colonel Page, the predecessor of Mr. Lewis, had *never* more than *seven* revenue agents; the average number not exceeding *four*. In July, 1849, Mr. Lewis had *nineteen;* in September, *thirty-one*, the average number ranging between *twenty and thirty!* These officers are employed by the Collector on the certificate of the Surveyor that they are necessary. Mr. Lewis is fortunate in having a second in the person of Mr. Norris. See for proof of the above returns, in the office of Register of Customs.

And now I have done with Mr. Lewis. In the recent investigation, the accusers were confined by the instructions of the Examiner to pooof of the facts set forth in the charges which had been preferred against him; and they were not permitted to go beyond them. The accused, however, was not confined, it would seem, to limits so circumscribed, being not only permitted to defend himself against the charges preferred, but to travel out of the record to assail me. Nor was he stopped there. He was permitted to concoct a libel, and without a word of proof to sustain the charges which it contains, to make it a part of the proceedings. I do not complain of this. On the contrary, I rather rejoice, that calumnies, which have long been whispered in private, have at length been made public, and the opportunity of repelling them afforded me. This controversy has been of Mr. Lewis' own seeking; and if the result has been an exposure of his baseness, the fault is his own.

NOTE.—The foregoing is the original draft of Mr. Cooper's Reply to Mr. Lewis' Narrative, and was prepared before any part of the testimony, taken before the Commissioner had been seen by him. Since its preparation, one or two extracts from the testimony have been inserted, and some other unimportant alterations made.

APPENDIX.

(B.)

Pottsville, May 10th, 1849.

To W. D. Lewis, Esq., Collector, &c.

Sir:—

Mr. George Read, of the county of Philadelphia, is an applicant for the office of Weigher in the Custom House, and it would afford me great pleasure to learn of his appointment. Mr. Read is an active Whig, who has rendered important services to the party, not only in the last but in previous campaigns; and is well qualified to discharge the duties of the post which he is seeking. He is a gentleman for whose appointment I am anxious, *provided it can be made in pursuance of the proposition contained in my other letter to you of this date.*

Very respectfully,
Your obedient servant,
(signed,) JAMES COOPER.

(C.)

Pottsville, May 10th, 1849.

Sir:—

Not less than one hundred persons have addressed me from different sections of the State, requesting recommendations to you, for sundry stations in your gift as Collector of the Port of Philadelphia. There are some *ten* of this number, who in addition to abundant qualifications have rendered important services to the Whig party, in the last and previous campaigns. If I can have the naming of *that number*, I will endeavour to present such persons as will be at once deserving and competent.

Two or three of the places should afford salaries of $1500 a year ; one or two of $1200; the remainder of from $800 to $1100, or thereabouts. If you can consent to this, inform me as early as your convenience will permit. *If you should do so*, I will begin by naming George Read for the situation of Weigher, for whose appointment I am anxious. If my proposal should not be complied with, there will be no harm done.

Very respectfully and truly yours,
(signed,) JAMES COOPER.

Wm. D. Lewis, Esq., Collector, &c.

(1.)

Philadelphia, May 12th, 1849.

Hon. James Cooper, U. S. Senator, Pottsville,—

Dear Sir: Mr. South did me the pleasure to hand me this morning, the two letters with which you were good enough to charge him for me.

My strong desire is that no errors shall be made in our early movements, and I shall therefore be very glad to have an opportunity of a personal interview with you here, as soon as you may find it convenient to see me.

Yours, very truly,
WM. D. LEWIS.

(2.)

Pottsville, May 15, 1849.*

WM. D. LEWIS, Esq., Collector,—

Dear Sir: I have this moment received your favor of the 12th inst., and cannot understand what you mean, when you say, "my strong desire is, that no errors shall be committed in our early movements."

Since writing to you, I have had information which leads me to believe, that I acted hastily, if not imprudently, in making the request and suggestions, which I did.

If the request just referred to, be in the slightest degree embarrassing, I beg you to think no more of it. Perhaps the better way is to withdraw it, if it be likely to lead to error in any movement. I therefore request you to return me my several letters of the 10th inst., or at least not to consider the recommendations.

Very respectfully, yours, JAMES COOPER.

---

* The above is the original draft. The copy sent Mr. Lewis may not be *verbatim* the same, but does not differ in any material part.

(3.)

Philadelphia, May 17, 1849.

Hon. JAMES COOPER, U. S. Senator, Pottsville,—

Dear Sir: Your favor of the 15th inst. reached me duly.

So incessant has been my occupation since I received notice of my appointment, in receiving during all my working hours applicants for office and their papers—and their name is legion—that I have been entirely unable to take up the subject of the patronage at all thus far. How soon this press may measurably cease I know not, for yesterday it was as heavy as on any previous day.

It would be very agreeable to me, however, if you could make it convenient to give me the pleasure of a personal interview with you soon; and in the meantime to furnish me with the names of those of your friends in whom you feel a particular interest in connection with places here.

If you can be one of a numerous party of political gentlemen, whom I this day invite to a social meeting at my house on Saturday evening next, at 8 o'clock, I shall be particularly gratified.

Very respectfully and truly yours, WM. D. LEWIS.

(F.)

Philadelphia, May 30, 1849.

Hon. JAMES COOPER, Pottsville.

DEAR SIR:—

I hand you herewith a notification of the appointment of Henry J. Schreiner, Esq., of Franklin county, which you will oblige me by giving its proper direction. *This is the gentleman in whom I understood you to feel a particular personal interest.*

And I beg leave to state further, that in consequence of the urgency with which you have advocated the appointment of George Read, Esq., to the highly responsible post of Weigher, I have in like manner, this day appointed him against the strongest and most general opposition I have ever witnessed here, on any like occasion. I mention this fact, not meaning to imply that I merit any particular praise for resisting the remonstrances of many powerful and highly valued friends in this instance, but merely that you may know that I am fully aware of the consequences likely to ensue from my determination to oblige you in making this appointment.

Very resepctfully and truly yours,

(signed) WM. D. LEWIS.

(X.)

Philadelphia, April 9th, 1851.

DEAR SIR:—

I have read in manuscript, that part of your reply to the Narrative of Wm. D. Lewis, Esq., which refers to two interviews you and I had with Gen. Taylor, in the month of March, 1849, the latter at his own request, communicated through Col. Mitchell of St. Louis. The statements made by you are correct; whenever it shall become necessary, I have additional testimony in my possession to confirm the accuracy of this statement.

I remain, dear Sir,
Your friend,
J. RANDALL.

(O.)

Extract of a Speech, delivered by Hon. Lewis C. Levin, at Southwark Hall, in May, 1849.

"Look what I have done for you. I had Roberts, a full blooded Native, appointed Marshal. I had Ashmead appointed District Attorney; and Sloanaker, the Naval Agent. This, I have done for you. Nay, more, before I would allow Wm. D. Lewis to be appointed Collector, I made him pledge himself to me, that he would select one half Natives to fill the offices. And so, too, with Post Master White; he made the same promises. Lewis is a Native, for last fall, when I was running for Congress, he gave me $250 towards my election, and worked hard for me. The lamented Grover gave $300. If you should be disappointed in getting office in the Custom House, or Post Office, there is the U. S. Marshal, who is a good Native, and has about sixty offices to give out. Besides, the Navy Yard and the Arsenal must be cleared out. . . . . These men shall redeem their pledges to me. Why the Whigs are abusing me now, and say, only see how much that scoundrel Levin has done at Washington."

(Y.)

Letter addressed to Hon. James Cooper, Pottsville.

Philadelphia, May 15, 1849.

MY DEAR FRIEND:—

I drop you a line in great haste, to say that Mr. Weaver and myself called to see Mr. Lewis and Henry White. They are both friendly, and disposed to give you all you ask for.

Mr. Lewis said he had written to you, and expected you to come to the city.

I beg and pray you to keep perfectly cool and calm upon this subject, and do not listen to hasty advisers. All that I have at heart, is your honor and political fame.*

Do come down in a day or two. Squire Jones goes to see you to-morrow. He is a good and discreet adviser.

In great haste,
G. W. SOUTH.

Write Henry White. He is favorable to Read, and says you can carry him.

---

* Why so apprehensive that Mr. Cooper would listen to hasty advisers against Read, if he was so urgent, as is alleged, in his solicitations for Read's appointment? The fear expressed in this letter, is another evidence that there existed a conspiracy to hold him to his recommendation, and right or wrongfully make him bear the odium of Read's appointment.

(G.)

Washington, January 30, 1850.

Gentlemen: You and the Hon. Lewis C. Levin, together with Lieut, Parke of the Army, were at my room at the National Hotel about the period of the meeting of Congress, and the conversation turning on the conduct of Mr. Lewis as Collector of the Port of Philadelphia, and the propriety of his confirmation by the Senate, Mr. Levin remarked in substance, that Mr. Lewis could not have done otherwise than he did in view of the circumstances of the case—that he was obliged to retain many Democrats in office, and was therefore unable to do what he desired for his political friends; but that as soon as he was confirmed by the Senate he could and would provide for them.

If this statement accords with your recollection, say so briefly on the opposite page.

Respectfully and truly yours,
JAMES COOPER.

The Honorables A. J. Ogle and C. W. Pitman.

House of Representatives, February 12, 1850.

Hon. James Cooper,—

Dear Sir: Our recollection of the conversation to which you refer in the foregoing letter accords substantially with your statement.

Respectfully yours,
A. J. OGLE,
C. W. PITMAN.

(I.)

Philadelphia City, SS.:

Lane Schofield, of the City of Philadelphia, being sworn on his oath, saith: That at the instance and request of William D. Lewis he was authorized to make bets for said Lewis, that he, Lewis, would be confirmed by U. S. Senate as Collector for the Port of Philadelphia. That he did make one bet for and on account of said Lewis of two hundred dollars, as the Agent of the said Lewis, that he, Lewis, would be confirmed as Port Collector as above stated. That this deponent has made several bets, not from political causes or considerations, but depending solely on the doctrine of chances. That James Cooper, U. S. Senator, is almost an entire stranger to this deponent, and never advised or knew anything of this deponent's bets—this deponent having made bets on his own judgment and calculation of chances, and not expecting sympathy or favor from any quarter in or out of Congress. That every body knows there are two sides, two parties to a bet—the one *for* and the other *against* the happening of some event. That thousands of dollars are staked on the one side that Lewis will be confirmed, and the men thus betting on the events are principally Custom House officers and retainers. That the men who have taken these bets—the opposite side—that Lewis will not be confirmed are men like this deponent, who, independent of political considerations, bet against the Custom House challengers, because they think that they shall win their bets. That this deponent, if the Senate of the U. States in Executive Session, should desire his presence, will cheerfully attend their request and unfold fully and prove by others the truth of the foregoing statement.

LANE SCHOFIELD.

Sworn and subscribed, the first day of August, 1850, before me.
JOEL JONES, Mayor.

We certify that the above, Lane Schofield, is a man of character and integrity, and has been for seventeen years a City Commissioner of Philadelphia, elected by the Councils.

AD. TRAQUAIR,
President of the City Commissioners.
ARMON DAVIS,
Alderman.

WILLIAMS OGLE, Alderman.

Affidavit of A. S. Hobbs, Esq., relative to a bet with Geo. J. Weaver, on or about the 1st of August, 1850:

City of Philadelphia, ss.:
Personally appeared before me, the subscriber, Mayor of the City of Philadelphia, A. S. Hobbs of said city, who being duly sworn according to law, saith, that on or about the first day of August instant, this deponent made a bet of five hundred dollars with George J. Weaver, on the confirmation of Wm. D. Lewis, as Collector of the Port of Philadelphia; he, the said Weaver, betting that said Wm. D. Lewis would be confirmed by the United States Senate in Executive Session as Collector aforesaid.

A. S. HOBBS.

Sworn and subscribed before me, August 31st, 1850,

JOEL JONES,
Mayor of the City of Philadelphia.

(Z.)

Philadelphia, Dec. 17, 1849.

Hon. James Cooper,—

Dear Sir: In compliance with my promise to you, and in pursuance of your request, made through our mutual friend, Sanderson, who was with me this morning, I now inclose with this the paper headed "Our Ticket and its Success,"* which was written for the "News," and in certain substantial particulars relating to persons therein named (the Collector and one of his personal friends), *required* to be inserted therein editorially.

I received it from Mr. Lewis, the fair copy as it now is *verbatim et literatim*, having been furnished in lieu of the original, retained by him. I have fastened the sheets together with eyelets since, which is the only change; and it has remained in my possession since.

* * * * *

Very respectfully,
Your ob't. servant,
CHARLES GILPIN.

---

* OUR TICKET AND ITS SUCCESS.

The nominations for City and County Officers having, as we have already stated, now been made by the friends of the National and State administrations, it behooves every Whig to buckle on his armor, and enter manfully into the contest with the firm determination of winning the victory.

Can any higher motives be urged upon our friends to incite them to exertion than the momentous issues, affecting every member of society, which are involved in the present struggle?

We must bear in mind that it is no longer a question of individual preference as to candidates: that matter has been decided according to established usage, and many among us, as must always be the case, have been disappointed that the choice did not fall upon those in whom we felt the most personal interest. The contests for places on the various tickets among our political brethren has, this season, been more animated than usual. We have had an unusual number of highly respectable competitors for the prizes, and, of course, a larger number of unsuccessful ones than perhaps on any former occasion.

It has, however, always been the boast of the Whigs party, that it was actuated by principles on which it believed the welfare of the country to depend; and that in its exertions to attain power, it had higher objects in view than mere party spoils. If this boast be true, as we firmly believe, now is the time to prove it by every advocate of those principles, rallying to the support of the nominees of the friends of General Taylor and W. F. Johnston. Their names will be found at the head of our editorial column. The arts of the enemy intended to distract and defeat us, are numerous, and we beg to caution our friends against being deluded by them.

One of the most insidious is the *calumny* they have of late been industriously spreading, that the nominations for mayor and sheriff are to be viewed in the light of anti-administration, and *anti-Custom House* triumphs; and the former nomination in particular, as Mr. Gilpin was an unsuccessful applicant for the collectorship of this Port. But what of that? Was not Col. Swift, who failed to obtain the nomination for the mayoralty, also an unsuccessful applicant for the collectorship? Mr. Gilpin was an early and prominent friend of Gen. Taylor, and still is so, and will give to his administration a warm and hearty support, whether in or out of office. He is in fact the administration candidate, and how can his nomination, by a constituency so largely in favor of Gen. Taylor, be deemed a rebuke to that virtuous and eminent citizen now at the head of our Republic? As to the story of the nomination of Mr. Gilpin or Mr. Rothermel being *an anti Custom House triumph, we know that some of the warmest advocates of both those gentlemen are now in the enjoyment of places in that establishment conferred on them by Mr. Lewis, the present collector, and believe that a majority of his officers were opposed to the nomination, to the Sheriffalty, of the gentleman in whose favor were supposed to be Mr. Lewis' personal predilictions.* Nor have we heard it alleged, nor do we entertain the belief that the *collector exercised, or attempted to exercise, the slightest control over his subordinates in this matter, or in that of the mayoralty. We know that he has expressed himself satisfied with the nominations, and has avowed his determination to sustain them, a sentiment which does him more honor, if they be not exactly those he* would have preferred, and which *we commend to the imitation of others.*

One word more on this subject before we leave it. Assuredly Mr. Lewis was not our choice for the post he now occupies, and some expressions may have found place in our columns in regard to him, *which we would have excluded on calmer reflection;* it is therefore that *we feel it to be the more our duty to do him justice on the present occasion*, and we take pleasure in saying, that when all the difficulties of his position at the time of his induction into office are considered, *we are of opinion that he has shown, upon the whole, great independence, impartiality, and judgment in the distribution of the public patronage under his control*, and has probably given as much general satisfaction in that respect as any of the other gentlemen who were spoken of for the place could have done.

Mr. Lewis' good sense and his just appreciation of the greatness of the stake at issue, will doubtless prevent the stories to which we have alluded, and another even more absurd one, viz., *that the omission to return one or more of his prominent friends as Ward Delegates was meant as a blow at him, or any special slight to them*, from having *any influence upon his mind.* The gentlemen alluded to are among the most valuable members of our party, known as well for their liberality as their indefatigable zeal in promoting the good cause; and who cannot, we are sure, be swayed from their duty, because in some particular instance a favorite candidate, through extraordinary exertions, succeeded in his own ward in electing other persons as delegates who were more certainly than they in favor of his nomination.

Let us then from this time henceforward move on in one unbroken phalanx, to the old war cry of TAYLOR, JOHNSTON, and FILLMORE, until our ears are again saluted by the glad shouts of victory.

Friends, that victory is certain if we but do our duty: the Locofoco battalions are already in disorder. Distrust and dissatisfaction pervade their ranks. Let us now achieve a victory over them more glorious, as it will be far more important in its results than the last. We have made GENERAL TAYLOR President, shall we now basely desert him? Whig principles have made an immense advance in the late elections of those benighted regions of Alabama and Maine, and shall PENNSYLVANIA, so lately redeemed, now falter?

Will she not support the Chief Magistrate whom she has elected?

If she should now fail what chance will there be for a modification of the Tariff, to suit her interests? None—not the slightest. Think of this fellow laborers in the good work, think of the importance of securing the control of your City and County government, of your Canal Commissioner, who is to be your sentinel over the management of our public works; and lastly, and above all things think of your legislative ticket, upon the success of which depends the character of the new Apportionment Bill. Remember that if we suffer ourselves now to be defeated, such a result will bind our glorious Commonwealth for seven years more *to the car of that worse than Juggernaut idol, Locofocoism.* Whigs, shall this be? It remains only for you to say IT SHALL NOT.

www.ingramcontent.com/pod-product-compliance
Lightning Source LLC
LaVergne TN
LVHW011119110826
845150LV00008B/2188
* 9 7 8 1 4 2 5 5 0 6 4 9 0 *